The Eye Drop Killer : Lana Sue Clayton

Jessi Dill

Published by Trellis Publishing, 2021.

While every precaution has been taken in the preparation of this book, the publisher assumes no responsibility for errors or omissions, or for damages resulting from the use of the information contained herein.

THE EYE DROP KILLER : LANA SUE CLAYTON

First edition. June 28, 2021.

Copyright © 2021 Jessi Dill.

ISBN: 979-8224353521

Written by Jessi Dill.

THE EYEDROP KILLER LANA SUE CLAYTON

JESSI DILL

When Lana Sue Clayton's husband, Steven, was found dead July 21, 2018, in the foyer of his expansive South Carolina mansion, authorities initially assumed he'd died during a fall down the stairs.

Everyone knew Steven adored his wife – even after she'd "accidentally" shot a crossbow at his head while he was asleep, none of their friends or neighbours suspected that the incident had been intentional. After Steven had survived the bizarre shooting with a fairly minor surface wound, he even managed to convince the local police investigating the incident that it was completely by accident, likely related the chronic sleeping disorder Lana Sue had been diagnosed with.

And she'd played the role of grieving wife perfectly after her husband was found dead in the couple's lakefront home. She told investigators that for days before his death, Steven had been complaining about vertigo – dizziness, headaches, and nausea. Lana Sue, a 52 year old nurse who worked at the VA in nearby Charlotte, seemed devastated by the loss of her husband.

"[Lana Sue] seemed like a sweet lady," said Ken Sanford, a friend of the couple's who also lived on Lake Wylie. "Steven was very proud of her accomplishments."

In August, the backyard of the palatial home – a lovingly restored and incredibly expensive replica of the famous Mt. Vernon residence formerly inhabited by George Washington – hosted the couple's equally devastated friends for Steven's funeral.

An entrepreneur, a visionary, and a strategist

A native of Florida, Steven Clayton had retired in the mid-1990s after he'd founded, owned, and operated a company called Physical Therapy Resources. According to Steven's obituary, the company eventually grew to open branches throughout the United States. However, Steven was better known for his generous spirit and positive personality.

"[Steven] was genuinely a kid at heart – energetic, fun, and always ready to lead the next adventure," his obituary read. "His exuberance for life, his captivating stories, and his irreverent sense of humor will be greatly missed by all who knew him."

As a former wrestling coach, Steven was good with kids and loved teaching. Throughout his life, he pursued opportunities to act as a mentor for children – in sports as well as in other areas. He also served on the editorial board of the Lake Wylie Pilot, all the way up until the local weekly newspaper ceased production in 2016.

And he was well liked around the community. Steven would frequently stop by the Bagel Boat, owned by Lake Wylie resident Frank Keefe, to enjoy a hot pastrami sandwich and visit with his friends and neighbours. According to his obituary, he loved wine, cigars, music, world travel, and Guinness and Sadie – his two Italian greyhounds.

According to his obituary, Steven had graduated from Miami Military Academy and Miami Springs Senior High School, where he'd been a celebrated athlete in a number of sports – including track, football, and Greco-Roman wrestling. From there, the obituary stated, he'd overcome "childhood hardships and adversity" thanks to his "indomitable spirit" to accomplish greater things.

"He was an entrepreneur, a visionary, and a brilliant business strategist who had a passion for learning and critical thinking," reads the obituary. "He continuously challenged himself to greater levels of success, while helping others along."

It seemed no one would want Steven Clayton dead – it was clear he'd simply had an accident on the stairs of his upscale home, and the unfortunate loss had left the community stunned. But things became even more shocking when police received the results of the toxicology report.

The results were unusual. According to the report, Steven's blood had contained a fatal level of a chemical called tetrahydrozoline – an ingredient included in typical over the counter eyedrops, used to whiten red eyes. While the chemical is also included in nasal sprays, swallowing even a small amount can cause seizures, cease breathing, and even induce comas.

Poison is no joke

In 2013, Wired reported that the chemical's effectiveness comes from the way "compounds bind to receptors in the sympathetic nervous system, altering signals to the vascular system, triggering the change." And the 2005 film Wedding Crashers helped popularize an urban legend that swallowing Visine will result in violent diarrhea.

But in real life, the damage caused by the chemical is no joke. A former Pizza Hut manager, Ginger Watson, was working at the restaurant in 2011 when an angry co-worker used the drops to spike her drink. Although she experienced a number of unpleasant symptoms, Watson managed to survive the incident.

"Chills, sweats, nausea, vomiting, diarrhea – I felt awful," she said in an interview with Inside Edition. "If I had an underlying medical condition or if I had gotten a little more of the drug, I could have been seriously injured or died."

The chemical can be purchased cheaply, and can be found at most drug stores or medicine cabinets – leading to products like eye drops and nasal sprays being used in several high-profiling poisonings over the past ten years.

A woman in Long Island received a three-year probation in 2008, after she used the chemical to spike her roommate's drink. In 2012, after almost killing his father by dumping two full bottles of Visine into his glass of milk "because he thought his dad was mean and wanted to make him pay," a man from the Cleveland area was punished with five years in prison. Charges were filed against a Wyoming teenager, who had poured around 20 bottles of the product into her stepmother's coffee and tea over a four month period in 2013. And in California, during that same year, a man was arrested after he'd used Visine to spike his girlfriend's drink after they'd had a big fight.

A 22 year old woman was arrested in 2014 in Thurmont, Maryland, on the charges of aggravated assault and endangering the welfare of children. According to a police report, the woman had confessed to the authorities that she'd been poisoning her three year old son with small amounts of Visine – putting drops into both his water bottle and his juice bottle. The boy had been admitted to the hospital a few times, but hadn't succumbed to the poison. When her one year old son got a hold of the spiked drink and consumed it, he became very ill – and the mother was forced to tell police what had happened. She eventually pleaded guilty to six counts of aggravated assault of a victim less than six years old, and one count of endangering the welfare of a child.

Other reports of the dangerous effects of ingesting eye drops have been publicized as far back as 1996, when a two year old child consumed between two to three milliliters of Visine drops. The toddler became "dangerously lethargic," according to Snopes, and was "unresponsibve to every stimulus except deep pain." The fact-checking website goes on to state that the child was able to successfully recover from the incident thanks for prompt medical attention, "but not before enduring intubation and two days' worth of mechanically-assisted breathing."

And the substance has frequently been used by "practical jokers" looking for a quick way to prank someone. A clerk at a Whole Foods market spiked a customer's wheat grass smoothie with a bottle of Visine in 1995. The customer subsequently fell violently ill, and spent several days in the hospital suffering from acute pain and a range of concerning medical issues. The clerk was fired, and the market eventually settled for an undisclosed sum after the customer filed a $1-million suit against the store.

A high school student in Southern California put a few drops of the chemical in a teacher's water bottle in October 2003, hoping to force the instructor to suffer severe diarrhea. Fortunately for the teacher, other students confessed to having seen the student committing the act and removed the compromised liquid before their teacher could consume it – and the student responsible was subsequently charged with tampering with a drink with intent to cause harm.

A few years later, five students at a Wisconsin high school attempted to pull the same prank on a classmate. In 2006, after drinking from a water bottle spiked with eye drops, a student was hospitalized for several days with symptoms including a dangerously low heart rate and blood pressure. The jokers were charged with counts of battery and disorderly conduct – and after pleading "no contest," they were given sentences of 18 months' probation and 60 hours of forced community service.

A charge of first degree assault was handed down to a Missouri woman in January of 2009, after she'd dumped half of a bottle of eye drops into a cup of tea she'd prepared for her husband – in an attempt to kill her spouse. He subsequently told investigators that he'd been suffering from stomach problems for a couple of months, and police learned from poison control personnel that ingesting even a relatively small amount of Visine "would put a person in a coma with several other serious symptoms. And in April 2017, a woman in Utah was found to have poisoned her husband over the course of several months – which police were beginning to suspect had happened to Steven Clayton, as well.

Devoted to her

Still curious about the state of the couple's relationship after the previous incident with the crossbow, deputies brought Lana Sue Clayton in to discuss the results of the report. They were also suspicious after Lana Sue had attempted suicide just weeks after Steven's backyard funeral – and only one day before her arrest.

According to police documents, Lana Sue confessed to the murder as soon as she was confronted with the evidence. Immediately, she was charged with homicide and malicious tampering of food.

"We don't have a clear cut reason why she committed the crime that she did, or what kind of motive she had," said Trent Faris, a spokesman for the York County Sheriff's Office. "She revealed that she used the liquid which is known normally [as] eye drops, and put it in his food – and she did that without his knowledge."

While Lana Sue has yet to enter a plea, it is alleged that she used the tetrahydrozoline to slowly poison her husband over the course of three days, by putting droplets of the chemical in his drinking water and in his meals between July 19 and 21.

Steven's family was distraught over the news that his wife was responsible for the murder, and released a statement saying they were "shocked and mortified at the cause of his death."

"All of our family and friends know how much he loved his wife, Lana, and how devoted he was to her," the statement read. "We are all still trying to process this."

The couple had spent eight years together. While Steven was well-known for his "big personality," Lana Sue was quieter – a regular member of a neighbourhood bible study group who tended to stay out of the spotlight.

In 2010, however, she'd opened up a bit on social media. A Facebook post from March of that year includes a comment from Lana Sue, claiming that Steven had been unfaithful to her at some point.

"My husband is not a drunk, he had an affair. However, he is the father of my children and my kids look at my Facebook," she wrote. "I do appreciate the support though."

The account has since been deleted, but reveals that there may be a motive for murder, after all – if the post refers to Steven, at all. The couple had only been married for eight years at the time of Steven's death in 2018, which makes it entirely possible that the husband she referred to in the Facebook post was the man she'd been married to before meeting Steven.

Prosecutors have also begun digging deeper into the crossbow incident, which could bring about some additional charges Lana Sue will have to face.

"He did not believe she was trying to kill him."

According to the incident report, Lana Sue had gone to the York County Sheriff's Office on May 30, 2016, to tell deputies that she'd accidentally shot her husband earlier that morning. Steven had been sleeping, she said, while she'd been attempting to load the weapon in her bedroom.

"She stated that the two sleep in separate beds," noted a police report taken at the time of the incident.

She was struggling to get the weapon to load properly, according to her statement, and grew frustrated and tired. She went upstairs to Steven's room with the crossbow in tow.

"She stated that she sat it up against a night stand and went to get into the bed, and realized her husband was already occupying that bed," stated the report. When Lana Sue got up to head into a different bedroom, she reached over to grab the crossbow – and as she picked it up, "it accidentally went off and struck her husband in the back of the head."

Steven woke up yelling, bleeding from his head. With significant experience as a nurse, Lana Sue immediately began administering aid to his wound. When authorities followed up with Steven, he told them he was just fine – the shooting was completely unintentional, he assured them.

"He told [the officer] he did not believe she was trying to kill him, but she has problems sleeping at night and sleep walks," read the police report.

But Lana Sue mentioned something that shone a different light on the incident. While she claimed he'd never "hit her," Lana Sue confessed to the police that her husband's "mood swings" had become mentally abusive.

"She advised that he has mood swings, and one moment he is nice to her and the next moment he can be cruel towards her," police stated in the report. "She stated that he rants and berates her, but has never hit her. Both [Lana Sue and Steven] stated the incident was accidental."

With that, the shooting was officially ruled as an accident.

"During the investigation, no intent to commit a crime was found," read the case report. "Incident was unfounded."

With that, the case was closed. According to family friend Lauren Stover, there had been no outward indications of any type of marital problems or abuse in the couple's history – nothing that would suggest that the police should invest additional manpower into an investigation.

Once Lana Sue confessed to poisoning her husband, however, the crossbow attack was viewed in an entirely new light.

"We are making a comprehensive review of all events in the relationship between the defendant and the victim," said prosecutor Kevin Brackett. "We will be taking a look at the relationship and the 2016 incident."

"The missus had poisoned him."

It was easy for people to believe that the shooting had been unintentional – and that Steven's death had been caused by a fall down the stairs. When it was revealed that Lana Sue had been slowly poisoning her husband with eye drops, their friends and neighbours admitted that they'd never seen it coming.

"All of us that knew Steve loved Steve. His family. His friends. Everyone is shocked over this horrible death," said Stover. "I don't even think Steve had any clue that eventually he would meet his demise by Lana. I don't think he had a clue."

According to Stover, the couple's friends and family had even mourned Steven's death with Lana Sue in the weeks leading up to her arrest – without realizing that not only had Steven been murdered, but that Lana Sue had been the one to do it.

"They didn't have any inkling at all that she was plotting against him," she said. "They looked like a normal couple, as far as the family was concerned."

"We were told he fell down the stairs," Stover added. "We thought that's how he died – nobody saw this coming. We're shocked and mortified over the cause of his death, for him to be dying such a horrible way and being such a loving human being."

Neighbours were equally confused and surprised. According to Deborah Pollard, who lives near the couple in Clover, the entire situations "just makes no sense." And neighbour Sean Magan couldn't believe a poisoning could happen in the Lake Wylie community – "Somebody does something like that? That's crazy."

Frank Keefe, owner of the Bagel Boat restaurant Steven visited regularly, said Lana Sue was "stoic" during the commemoration of Steven's life hosted in the backyard of the couple's mansion. According to Keefe, the ceremony was "peaceful" and "beautiful" – a fitting tribute to Steven's memory.

"[He was] well-respected," Keefe said. "Family loved him. I saw a lot of love, a lot of kindness. There were tears of joy at this event, which just makes it that much more stunning when we received the call saying that the missus had poisoned him."

By outward appearances, Keefe said, the couple "seemed to have it all." Steven had built himself up from working as a labourer while he was in college to an entrepreneur – owner of a national company. When he was able to retire in 1995, he spent his time traveling the world.

"Steven was truly a magnanimous man, and his broad circle of friends was infinitely diverse," read his obituary, written by one of his four sisters. "He enjoyed spending time in the company of gardeners and janitors, as much as he did with captains of industry and finance moguls. He had no mere acquaintances, as everyone he befriended became part of his enormous, extended family."

Steven married Lana Sue in November of 2013 – it was the second marriage for both of them. Lana Sue had filed for bankruptcy in 2010, but seemed to have her life back on track. She was working as a nurse for the United States Department of Veteran Affairs, and – according to a Nov. 3, 2013, Facebook post made by one of her nieces – had finally found "a man that loves her like she deserves."

With Steven, Lana Sue began enjoying a much different lifestyle. Steven was a world traveler who loved the finer things – cigars, good wine, and collecting expensive art pieces. But just five years later, Steven suddenly died on the floor of their palatial foyer.

According to what Lana Sue told deputies who responded to the waterfront home that day, Steven had been ill over the last several days – his vertigo was so bad, she claimed, that he hadn't even left the bedroom unless it was absolutely necessary. In an effort to give her husband a break from doing the regular household chores, Lana Sue went to mow the expansive lawn by herself, leaving Steven upstairs to sleep. But when she came back inside after finishing her yard work, Lana Sue found her husband stretched across the floor, face down by the foot of the stairs.

In her statement to police, Lana Sue said she attempted to turn her husband over, to see if he was breathing. When she was unable to flip him over due to his heft, she left the house and went to a neighbour's to get help. Soon after, both EMS and the coroner arrived on the scene.

The police report states that, initially, authorities "believed the event to be cardiac in nature, due to the physical evidence and the condition of the deceased." However, because of Steven's relatively young age and his apparent "lack of medical history," deputies also alerted a York County detective, who began investigating the death.

Then, police were dispatched to the couple's home once again, just a few weeks later.

The distraught widow

On August 30, the day before Lana Sue would be arrested for her role in her husband's death, she attempted to take her own life. Police, alerted to a potential suicide by a neighbour, immediately responded.

The last her neighbours had seen of her was the night before, they explained. She'd seemed distraught when she stopped by at around 9:30 p.m. on August 29, and she'd asked if her neighbours could watch her dogs.

Mike Kelly, another Lake Wylie resident, told the police he'd seen notes from Lana Sue that seemed suicidal in tone. And when the officers reached the back of the massive estate, they quickly recognized the smell of natural gas. According to the police report, as soon as the door was opened, the officers were "overwhelmed by the fumes."

"We tried to look around the house, but we could not breathe to do a full search of the home," read the report. "On the back deck, there were several suicidal notes on the table."

Police have not indicated whether or not the notes contained confessions or admissions of guilt by Lana Sue, regarding her role in her husband's death.

Once officials from the fire department arrived and shut off the gas to the home, firefighters accompanied a detective into the home – sporting oxygen masks to ensure their safety. Lana Sue was found lying on the bed, unconscious but still breathing. She was then transported to Rock Hill, where she was booked into the Piedmont Medical Center.

According to Trent Faris, spokesperson for the York County Sheriff's Office, police had spoken with Lana Sue about her possible involvement in her husband's death prior to the attempted suicide.

"She was brought in for questioning after the toxicology report came back," he explained.

Faris also noted that bottles of eye drops were found in the couple's home, which were picked up by investigators and taken into evidence.

The next day, Lana Sue confessed to putting eye drops in her husband's food and drink – and was subsequently arrested.

A bleak future

Now, the rest of Steven's family is trying to keep Lana Sue from obtaining any of her late husband's substantial assets. Per municipal records, the Lake Wylie home is worth upwards of $820,000 – and Steven owned another lot, adjacent to the couple's mansion, valued at an additional $385,000.

According to online property sites, the house is a "newly built, 1940s style Greek Revival home," which "sits on two acres of prime lakefront."

While Lana Sue was appointed the personal representative for the estate following her husband's death, Stover – with the help of Steven's immediate family – is working with a probate attorney to address the issue.

"They're not supporting any financial gain for someone who has actually been responsible for the termination of their brother's life," she said.

Currently, the situation remains unclear – what impact Lana Sue's arrest may have on the probate action, or how the estate of the late Steven Clayton will be disbursed among his beneficiaries.

Additionally, Lana Sue may be facing the death penalty if convicted by a jury. Under the current law in South Carolina, one of the aggravating factors that can be invoked by prosecutors to seek capital punishment is "killing by poison" – which Lana Sue has already confessed to be guilty of.

However, according to 16th Circuit Deputy Solicitor Willy Thompson, prosecutors hadn't made any decisions about the consideration of the death penalty as of September 2018 – it's still "far too early in the case," Thompson said.

In order for a death sentence to be handed down, the penalty has to be sought specifically by the prosecution. So far, according to 16th

Circuit Solicitor Kevin Brackett, there has been no case file submitted by the York County Sheriff's office, and "no discussions" have been had as to whether or not the prosecution may be viewing it as a possible capital case.

The process has been met with criticism from some – including Brackett. According to statements he has made to media in the past, the death penalty process in South Carolina is – in Brackett's words – a "sham" that involves drawn out appeals and other conflicts, leaving the families of the victims stuck in the court system for years – even decades.

As of September, Lana Sue has yet to hire a lawyer to represent her as she defends herself at trial, said officials with the York County Clerk of Court. She continues to remain incarcerated in the York County jail, where she is held without bond.

KILLER STRIPPER : THE TRUE STORY OF MECHELE HUGHES

JAMES MORRIS

Kent Leppink's death

Kent Leppink was a commercial fisherman from a relatively comfortable background. He had lived several places in Alaska by the time he settled down in Anchorage, and shared a house with Mechele Hughes and another man named John Carlin III.

His body was left on a hiking trail near Hope, Alaska, an hour from Anchorage. He was discovered by utility workers making their way to a job. But perhaps because of the conditions on that remote hillside, or because of the carefulness of the murderers, no physical evidence was found that could have tied anybody to the crime.

What little evidence there was, and common sense, pointed towards Mechele and Carlin, but not enough to bring them to trial. Leppink's death, however, was almost overshadowed by Mechele Hughes' story: a stripper who had perhaps had her boyfriend murdered in cold blood, by her lover. The salacious story gripped headlines around the country when the case went to trial, a full decade after the crime.

The murder

Details of what happened on the day of Kent Leppink's death are difficult to come by, and were only pieced together during the trial-which came after more than a decade of waiting.

What Kent Leppink may or may not have known, was that Mechele had been seeing at least two other men while living with him, including their housemate Carlin. There was also another man named Scott Hilke, who lived in California. According to allegations that later came out at trial, she had been engaged to them all at some point or another, and maintained relationships with all three at the same time.

On May 2nd 1996, Leppink was found dead courtesy of three gunshot wounds from a .44 calibre handgun. He had been shot at point blank range, and according to the pathologists' report had been murdered anywhere between 6 and 48 hours before his body was recovered.

Whether Mechele and Carlin kept their affair a secret is impossible to say, but perhaps it was the threat of it being revealed that led to Leppink's murder. This, at least, was what State Troopers investigating the case believed. They interviewed Hughes, Carlin and Hilke to try to get to the bottom of what had happened but couldn't definitively pin the crime on any one of them, nor on anybody else.

No charges were brought against Hughes, or against anybody else connected to the crime. And because of the lack of any new evidence coming to light, the case went cold.

A breakthrough after a decade

Michele finally faced court only ten years later, in October 2006. While no fresh physical evidence had been unearthed, the State of Alaska's cold case team- just three people, as it happens- had made a breakthrough during an interview with Carlin's son. He had been underage in 1996, and hadn't been allowed to speak to police. His testimony was so damning that charges were brought against both his father and Mechele Hughes.

The cold case team were also able to confiscate Kent's old computer, which gave them important clues going forward in the case. According to Betsy Leppink's interview with NBC in 2008, she described how information on the computer had been vital: "It held information that was very important to both trials," and she added that the technology to access the information simply hadn't been available all those years ago.

The team had recovered emails from the computer which heavily implied that Carlin and Hughes had lured Leppink out to Hope, Alaska that day. The pair had said that they were renting a cabin in the area, and invited Leppink along; but in reality, there was no cabin, no holiday, and no return home for Leppink.

Another startling piece of evidence was a stolen bronze statue, which John Carlin had kept through all the intervening years. "That was very, very big in the trial," Betsy said during her interview. At that point, it had been returned to Betsy and Ken, and sat in their living room. "She [Hughes] stole it from him. They found it just before Carlin's trial on his fireplace mantle in New Jersey." "On the back side of it, our son's name is printed on it," Ken added.

Based on both new and old evidence, as well as testimony from interviews, the cold case team concluded that Hughes had not murdered Leppink; she had persuaded Carlin to shoot him instead. This made her an accomplice, just as guilty and just as liable for his death. He was sent to a prison in Seward, Alaska.

The first trial, however, was of Carlin alone. Between March and April 2007 he was tried, found guilty and sentenced to life in prison. Carlin's conviction convinced prosecutors to go ahead with Hughes' case, because of her involvement in persuading Carlin to act.

A trial after twelve years

Her supposed motive had been money, as motives often are. Leppink's life insurance would have made Michele and Carlin millionaires, and prosecutors argued that this was all the temptation needed for them to kill him. The beneficiary of this insurance was changed only a few days prior to Leppink's death, however, so Hughes wouldn't have received any pay-out at all. Hughes argued that she had, in fact, tried to cancel the policy- not get the money for herself.

One important piece of evidence was a letter, written by Leppink shortly before his murder. In it he told his parents that if he were to die under 'suspicious circumstances', that it was probably Hughes and Carlin who were responsible. In the letter, he told his parents about Hughes' 'split personality' and that while 'the part [he] fell in love with is very beautiful' that his parents had 'to take Mechele down' and 'make sure she is prosecuted.'

The judge- Anchorage Superior Court Judge Philip Volland- allowed the evidence on the basis that it showed the jury how easy Leppink had been to manipulate, which was one of the central points of the case. Prosecutors had argued that Hughes used Leppink in an effort to gain his life insurance, and for this to have made sense, it was necessary to prove Leppink's naivety and easiness to manipulate.

Prosecutor Pat Gullufsen also brought Hughes' character into disrepute during the trial. He claimed that she had been trying her best to imitate the lead character from the movie 'The Last Seduction', where a woman kills her partner and pins the crime on her lover. And while the inclusion of this line of evidence was strange, and pushing the boundaries of what was allowed in court, the judge allowed the jury to consider it. Prosecutors also argued that Hughes had helped Carlin to wash the murder weapon after Leppink's shooting, cementing her guilt.

Her defence attorneys argued that the evidence brought to trial amounted to a witch hunt, and too much emphasis was placed on Hughes' character as opposed to her actions; before sentencing, Hughes had been subjected to two days of questioning and discussion of her past.

A nationally renowned psychologist, however, testified that Hughes showed none of the signs of personality disorders that can lead to aggression, nor did she show any signs of having overcome (or struggled to overcome) guilt from having murdered Leppink. This suggested that Hughes was completely innocent of having either murdered her fiancé, or planned his murder.

Throughout the trial, Hughes' husband had attended in support. During the judge's verdict, Dr. Linehan was sat behind Mechele, shaking his head at the judge's words.

Hughes was found guilty of Leppink's murder just over a year after the trial began, on October 22nd 2007. Early the next year, she was sentenced to a total of 99 years in prison. She was sent to Hiland Mountain Correctional Center, in Eagle River, Alaska.

Speaking with his wife after the trial, Dr. Linehan said that they would "appeal vigorously the decisions by Judge Volland during the trial." He continued, "...there's the Mechele that everyone who knows her and has been around her for years knows. And the Mechele that the prosecution invented, their narrative."

Judge Volland did at least concede that Hughes should be incarcerated close to her family in Washington, but that was scant comfort for the family who believed that the verdict was an extreme miscarriage of justice.

Who had Hughes become since 1996?

Mechele had become a completely different person since the case was first opened. Between Leppink's murder and Hughes' eventual trial, Mechele Hughes had become Mechele Linehan. She had married Dr. Colin Linehan after the events of the case, and settled down to a normal family life, and even earned a Master's degree. The couple had even had a daughter together, who was 8 years old at the time of the trial.

On March 8th, 2008 CBS's *48 Hours* aired a special on her case, with an exclusive interview. She told an entirely different story to the one which had been used against her. Speaking with reporter Susan Spencer, she said "I just feel like there is nothing I can do to make people believe me or make people like me... A witch I may be, but a psychopath I am definitely not."

"Anybody else that knew me or worked with me didn't feel that way," she says. "You tell me how a 22-year-old girl can make grown men do these things." She also spoke about against the attacks on her character: "The only person I agreed to marry was Scott [Hilke]," she said, and she had only agreed to pretend to be engaged for Leppink's parents.

"I think [Leppink] was gay...he could never tell his family he was gay....He was frantic," she told Spencer as a way of making sense of this situation. Her current husband, Dr. Colin Linehan, also spoke with CBS in that same interview. "This whole thing is surreal. [A] nerve-shattering, anxiety-provoking nightmare...the bottom line is that's not who she is." But Linehan still felt sorry for Leppink's parents over the loss of their son. "Their son is dead. You can't take back the dead. I have nothing but sympathy for them."

The other side of the story

The case had always remained fresh in the public imagination, as stories of women who kill often do. The question of Hughes' innocence or guilt made great TV. Her notorious case was featured on numerous TV cable shows, and the way it was portrayed was a world away from the seemingly genuine interviews the Linehan family gave on CBS.

Shortly after Hughes' conviction- on July 27th, 2008- it was featured in an episode of Dateline NBC, and the next year an updated version with new information was aired too. Soon after, Oxygen Network show Snapped showed a special on Hughes' case, as did Investigation Discovery on the ID Channel. The show was titled 'Love and Death in Alaska'. Hughes's case also featured on E! Network's Fatal Beauty: 15 Most Notorious Women, again in 2009.

But aside from profiles of the beautiful woman turned 'murderer', the parents of Kent Leppink told their story on national TV too. In 2008, the couple- along with their two sons, Craig and Ransom-

appeared on that same episode of Dateline NBC to give their version of the events of that night, twelve years ago.

It wasn't easy. "We are not naive people anymore," Betsy said. "We've been through too much and have seen too much. Today we still cry. It was horrendous hell." And they didn't mince their words nor hide their suspicions when they discussed Hughes: "She was engaged to four guys at one time," Ken told NBC.

Leppink's parents had always maintained that there was something strange about their son's life insurance policy, which had been bought for him (supposedly) by Hughes' family. "The day he called me that his bronze had been stolen, he said, 'Mom, Mechele's grandpa gave us our wedding gift. It's a million dollar insurance policy on my life,'" Betsy said in her NBC interview. "I said, 'Kent, that's insane. No grandpa buys the future husband of his granddaughter a million dollar life insurance policy.' We were scared to death. I said, 'Get out of there — you're in trouble.'"

They had only met Mechele once, but hadn't taken to her. Whatever it was- they couldn't quite put their finger on it- something wasn't right. "I didn't think that she loved him. She showed no sign of affection toward him," Betsy said. "And the drool was running right out of him. She was a beautiful young girl. By the time we were afraid for his life, it was just too late."

"He just didn't want to give up. He said, 'Mom, I want to give it one more chance.'"

They also discussed the letter that they had received from Kent- more of a package, really- and revealed more about it than had come out at trial. Their son had written that it was his "insurance policy", and he wrote that "If I didn't think that things could get a little 'rough' up here, I wouldn't have sent you this. It's not funny to talk about getting killed, but in today's world you have to expect anything."

Kent also told them to take care of his final affairs, and not dwell for too long on his death. But most importantly, he had asked of them to "take Mechele DOWN. Make sure she is prosecuted."

Prison time

Hughes' spent her time in prison wisely. She did her best to acclimatize herself to what was a completely different environment than the one she had been used to. Her first prison job was for 85c. an hour, sewing prison uniforms.

But she couldn't escape completely from prison life. She had to learn how to work the black market, like every other prisoner- but for her, she didn't want drugs or makeup. She mostly used the system to get fresh fruit and vegetables.

A couple of times she got in trouble- and ended up in solitary confinement- because of the goods she used for bartering, like chewing tobacco. But the rest of her time she spent in her own cell, as she wasn't required to share with anyone else.

Later on, to avoid the black market altogether, she got the privilege of being able to order food from Costco and used an iron to make herself paninis. It was small reminders of life on the outside like this that kept her sane, she said in later interviews. She would also pass her time reading magazines like the New Yorker, and whatever books her family and friends would send to her.

After a year in prison, she switched jobs. She became a prison janitor, working the night shift, so as to avoid the drama and conflict that came from working with others. She would work from 10:30pm to 6:30am each night.

Throughout her time in prison, she received letters: thousands of them, all from strangers. Speaking about them to the press, she described how only three of them had been negative; and she wrote back to as many as she could, even the 'hate mail'. She kept some of the letters and cards that she received, and decorated her cell with them.

The most difficult aspect of her imprisonment was being away from her daughter. She had been 8 years old when Hughes went to jail. "I had a woman tell me when I first got there that you could be a mom from jail," she later said; but she found it difficult nonetheless. It was her daughter that inspired her to keep going, and do everything she could to win her freedom.

Hughes' appeal

Hughes never gave up on her freedom, and she was right not to. Her conviction was fully overturned on February 5th, 2010, by the Alaska Court of Appeals. The reversal was based on the improper evidence that had been allowed to influence the jury's decision: testimony on the movie The Last Seduction, and the letter written by Leppink which was read out in court.

"The State's case against Linehan was circumstantial, and the evidence was subject to different interpretations and was hardly overwhelming," Appeals Chief Judge Robert Coats wrote. "We accordingly conclude that Linehan's conviction must be reversed."

"The State's ability to secure a guilty verdict hinged on convincing the jury to view a large number of ambiguous facts in the light most favorable to Linehan's guilt. In this situation, the evidence of Leppink's posthumous accusations may well have been the weight that tipped the jury's decision," Judge David Mannheimmer wrote.

The judgment was passed 3-0. "Many law-abiding people are drawn to characters in literature or in the cinema who are villainous or roguish—even though they would not dream of engaging in the same crimes or misdeeds," wrote Mannheimer on the topic of the inclusion of 'The Last Seduction' as a major point of the prosecution. Mannheimer also wrote in his statement that Leppink's letter alone would have been enough to overturn Hughes' sentence.

This was based on the fact that a murder victim's testimony doesn't allow for questioning of either the maker of that testimony, nor does it allow the accused to defend themselves against what is written. It's also emotional testimony, which can influence the jury negatively and take their mind away from the actual testimony, and the actual evidence, presented at trial.

'It is almost inevitable that the jurors would view Leppink's assertions as at least circumstantial proof of the matters asserted. In other words, the jurors would suspect that Leppink probably knew what he was talking about," according to the appeals court statement made after the decision was overturned. They also wrote that such evidence is particularly damaging in a case based almost solely on circumstantial evidence, as this one had been.

Hughes' three appeal lawyers, Jeff Feldman, Susan Orlansky and former Alaska Supreme Court Justice Alex Bryne, also brought up the fact that her job as a stripper should never have been brought up, for similar reasons, since it could have clouded the jury's judgment and made the case about her character and not the murder. However, the appeal judges dismissed this particular claim.

Carlin's story took another turn as well, when his sentence was overturned too, on January 21st 2015. But this reverse came far too late for him. He had been found found beaten to death by the other inmates at Spring Creek Correctional Center just a year after his initial incarceration. Nobody has ever been charged with his murder, and had maintained his innocence and his appeals until he died.

Release

The district attorney had two choices now that Hughes' sentence had been overturned: she could either be taken to the Alaska Supreme Court and retried, or set free. But on May 11th, 2010, it was decided that she could be released on $250,000 bail. This sum was far beyond the means of Hughes and her family, who couldn't even afford a bail bondsman at $25,000, or ten percent of the total.

Fortunately for Hughes, a Pennsylvanian businessman donated the necessary money. At the same time, local Anchorage strip club owner

Terry Stahlman had offered his premises as collateral against the sum, although this was rejected by Judge Volland.

The businessman, Brian Watt, is a CFO from Chester Springs, Pa. He donated the bail money because of his firm belief in Hughes' innocence, and expected absolutely nothing in return. He was quoted by the Alaska Dispatch News as saying that he wanted to see 'the process play itself out', and Hughes given another trial, but this time, a fair one.

His intention was far from a desire to be in the limelight, and in short newspaper interviews he expressed his desire to not give out details of his own life. "In the simplest sense, I'm an analyst. I build predictive models of consumer behavior for a living. I analyze complex situations for a living, and ... my conclusion (is) she is innocent. One hundred percent," he wrote in an email to the ADN.

"It was as if the Internet hyenas had gathered at the watering hole, and they were going to rip the flesh from her bones, no matter what she said or did," Watt said. At no point had he ever met Hughes, Leppink or Carlin- nor had he ever even been to Alaska. But his conviction and empathy were so firm that he decided to donate the money.

"The narrative that was being told, in the media, on blogs, and reader commentary on the Internet, took on a life of its own," he wrote in the email. "It appeared to me to be impossible for Mrs. Linehan to escape that pre-assembled story." In all fairness to Watt, the case had been overturned for just those reasons. But his donation was nevertheless remarkable.

Perhaps even more surprisingly, Watt wrote in the same email that it hadn't been the first time he had donated bail money to what he deemed to be worthy causes, although he refused to elaborate further. "I guess I could have saved all the money I spent over the years on these type of projects, and retired early but I never wanted to retire anyways, so it's all good," he told the ADN.

It had only been a short two and a half years since she had been sent to prison to begin with. The conditions of her bail were that she had to stay in the local area, and for all intents and purposes remain under house arrest until the date of her trial, which had been set for September that year.

Life goes on

On August 6th 2012, prosecutors finally decided that they would not send Hughes back to court to face trial again.

In speaking to the Alaska Dispatch News since her release, Hughes has expressed her regret at her youth, saying that she was reckless and manipulative in her early 20s, but that she had since changed, and that it had never made her a killer. She has given extensive interviews to newspapers since her release, describing her experience.

She did set some ground rules, however, for her interviews. In her interview with the Fairbanks Daily News-Miner, for instance, she said that the location of her new apartment couldn't be disclosed; but also she stipulated that she didn't want to talk about the case, on the advice of her new defense lawyers. She requested as well that the name of her daughter was not to be published.

Speaking with the Daily News, she spoke of how she felt after she was let go. She was met by her husband and daughter, and a court appointed custodian who helped her reintegrate into normal life. She had agreed with her family that she would stay in a small studio apartment to begin with, and it was in setting this apartment up that she spent most of her time in that first week.

"I had forgotten how soft a bed could be," she told the paper. In those first few days, she indulged in some of her favourite comfort food, a privilege she hadn't had in prison- avocado, mango and sushi. She spent the first week meeting with her family, her new team of lawyers, and just trying to be normal again.

On the topic of her public image, she told the Daily News "[m]y attorneys always told me to be stoic in court, even during the trial: 'Just be stoic.' So I'd sit there and try to be stoic. Which I laugh at now because that got twisted (into) 'Cold, manipulative bitch. Look at her.' No, I was being stoic, that was my stoic look. You got to either laugh or cry at the situation and crying does you no good."

The twisting of her public image had an effect on her that she was eager to speak out about. "You don't know what it's like to be told that you are the devil woman," she said. Her friends and family told her not to let her portrayal in the media affect her. "From the beginning people told me I'm too thin-skinned. 'You need to toughen up. Let it roll off your back like water, you're a duck,'" she said. "I thought I wanted to be like that, for it to not bother me. But it always did."

At the time of writing, Mechele Hughes operates a Laser Clinic in Tacoma, Washington.

SERIAL KILLING STRIPPER: THE TRUE STORY OF ROBYN LINDHOLM

CHELSEA CALBERT

Australia's Most Dangerous Woman

Robyn Lindholm was destined for fame. By the age of 14, this talented, beautiful young woman was already an up-and-comer in the world of Australian figure skating – competing in national ice-skating championships and even performing alongside Olympic legends Torvill and Dean, handpicked by the duo to participate in their sold-out Face The Music world tour.

However, it wasn't her talent on the ice that ensured Lindholm's name would appear on the front page of newspapers for years. Instead, this gorgeous femme fatale will be remembered as a murderer – and potentially, even a serial killer.

The Victorian Supreme Court finally sentenced 43-year-old Lindholm to 25 years in prison for the premeditated murder of her ex-boyfriend, Wayne Amey, in December of 2015 – but then, police began investigating the possibility that Lindholm was behind at least one other death, as well as the possible murder of another past lover.

"She had an uncanny ability to manipulate men," said Chief Crown Prosecutor Gavin Silbert QC, during one of Lindholm's trials.

Always daddy's girl

Born into a wealthy Melbourne family, Lindholm learned at an early age that her good looks and charm could get her anything she wanted. Even her father was powerless to resist. At the age of 11, Lindholm convinced him that she needed a pony. A few years later, a 14-year-old Lindholm demanded pricey skating lessons – and her dad never failed to indulge his daughter's every wish.

While Lindholm relied heavily on her appearance to get ahead, she grew up a fairly hardworking young girl. After excelling at Kilvington Grammar and even at an elite secondary college, Lindholm planned to attend Monash University to study a Bachelor of Science degree. Her love of horses had endured since childhood, and her passion for endurance riding led Lindholm to pursue a career working with animals.

Her bright future began to derail when she accepted a part-time job working in one of the high-roller rooms at the Crown Casino, the Mahogany Room. Even though Lindholm was just a hostess, her long legs and beautiful blonde hair caught the eye of "the Black Prince of Lygon Street." Alphonse Gangitano was an attractive and wealthy underworld crime leader, and Lindholm was unable to resist the allure of the handsome and powerful man's lifestyle of money, sex, and drugs.

Lindholm's demanding nature suited Gangitano just fine. Once again, she was treated like a princess – Gangitano was more than willing to indulge Lindholm's every whim and buy her whatever she desired. When Gangitano was eventually executed in his own home,

Lindholm would need to find another way to maintain the intoxicating lifestyle she'd gotten accustomed to – by whatever means necessary.

Simply Irresistible

While working in the Mahogany Room, Lindholm had developed a relationship with Alex Prelac – a regular customer of the exclusive high-roller room who owned the Simply Irresistible Stripping Agency. Lindholm had purchased her first small farm in Glenhope when she was only 23, and agreed to work part-time for Prelac's agency to help pay down her mortgage.

Stripping not only provided Lindholm with a steady income and the exciting lifestyle she was looking for – it also indulged her need to be the centre of attention. Her job with Simply Irresistible wasn't enough, though. Soon, Lindholm made the jump from stripping to working back in Melbourne's underworld as a highly-paid escort, going by the name "Collette."

John Elder, who worked as editor-in-chief of a magazine that routinely hired strippers for pranks and other comical roles, recalled meeting Lindholm when she was only 20 years old – "an ice-skating champion, newly dropped out of a science degree, moving into animal husbandry."

"She talked to me about her dream of owning her own place in the country, horses, a quiet life," he said. "There was nothing to suggest she'd end up burying one, maybe two boyfriends at the wished-for homestead."

Elder added that for Lindholm, stripping was a "means to a real-estate end," and that as soon as she was able to save enough money, she'd move on to her real passion of working with horses.

Soon after she started at the club, Lindholm struck up a close friendship with another stripper, Shari Davison. Davison was an exotic dancer who had previously worked as a circus trapeze artist, and who had just had a baby when she disappeared after leaving the Crown Casino on a Saturday morning in February of 1995. Her body has never been recovered, but investigations soon began to point to her good friend, Lindholm.

"There were so many rumours, ratbags, and depraved offshoots in our digging around," Elder said. "An inquest in 2001 found that Davison had a taste for drugs, booze, and bad men – and was pronounced mysteriously dead."

Apparently, in the weeks leading up to her disappearance, Davison had confessed to some close friends that she was "in serious trouble" with a gang of young Greeks – a gang which included standover man George Teazis, who had recently started seeing a stripper known as "Collette."

Teazis, also known as Templeton, had once been a member of a Richmond-based gang. The gang participated in the trading of weapons and amphetamines, dubbed the "plastic gangsters." Teazis fell head over heels in love with Lindhom, and even went as far to propose to her and move her into his home. However, he vanished in 2005, shortly after the engagement, and his body remains unfound.

A volatile situation

Two weeks prior to his disappearance, Teazis's brother received an upsetting phone call. Teazis was in tears, distraught over having just caught Lindholm in bed with, presumably, Wayne Amey. According to the brother, the couple had a "violent fight," and Teazis decided to leave Lindholm.

On the day Teazis disappeared, Lindholm had been out with a friend. When she came home, she claims the door was open and Teazis was gone. According to Lindholm, Teazis had sent a text at around 2:30am, stating that he was in some kind of trouble and would need a ride home, but she didn't know where he was.

Tearfully, Lindholm took to the press to express her pain and desire to locate her beloved fiancé. In the meantime, though, she moved all the furniture out of Teazis' home and claimed all of his assets – leaving a small box of toys for her fiancé's grief-stricken teenage son, Ross.

"Ross noticed that his father's F100 campervan was missing, along with his motorbike, a boat, a rear-projection television, jewellery, and other assorted goods worth an uncounted tens of thousands of dollars," said Elder. "Ross says he was so stunned at the time, he immediately went to a friend's home to settle himself. Later, he tried calling (Lindholm), to claim his father's belongings."

According to Ross, Lindholm eventually texted to tell him that she'd left some "clothes and his remote-controlled cars" in boxes on the doorstep. When Ross inquired about the vehicles, Lindholm replied that he would be "getting nothing ... and she forwarded her solicitor's details."

And while Lindholm made a show of crying for the press, Teazis' family members claimed that before getting in front of the cameras, Lindholm had been "laughing with her friend." After shedding some tears during the press conference and mourning the disappearance of her lover, she was "seen laughing again when it was over."

She also chose not to mention her new lover to the TV and newspaper reporters. Before Teazis' disappearance, Lindholm had started an affair with a gym owner named Wayne Amey. With Teazis out of the picture and her stripping career taking off, Lindholm was on track to get everything she ever wanted.

Lindholm reluctanty sold her Glenhope farm to purchase land with Amey, a 10-acre property near Bittern. This would give her plenty of space to pursue her lasting love of equestrianism and, eventually, begin breeding horses. Up until her arrest, Lindholm continued to enjoy endurance riding, and at the time Amey was killed, their property was home to eight beautiful – and expensive – Arabian horses.

Lady Macbeth in Lycra

Although Teazis' body was never recovered, Lindholm was formally charged with his murder in June of 2016. In 2005, police had conceded that it was possible that Teazis may not have wanted to ever be found – but since he hadn't used his mobile phone or accessed his bank accounts, they had "grave concerns."

According to police, Lindholm had convinced her new lover, Amey, to help her kill and dispose of her fiancé – a story that was somewhat corroborated by a strip club owner who had hired Amey as a personal trainer.

"He said (Teazis) was knocking Robyn around," she told Elder. "He kept saying he was going to kill (Teazis). It went on and on. It got scary and I stopped training with him."

The charge came just a few months after Lindholm was convicted of persuading another lover, Torsten "Toots" Trabert, to murder Amey. According to Elder, Lindholm and Amey were separating – and Amey had hoped for a settlement that would leave him half of the couple's rural property.

"Lindholm was angry, vengeful, and bitter over the break-up of her relationship with Amey and the loss of the farm, and he became anxious for his own safety," said a newspaper article published in The Sunday Age, discussing the case.

According to defence barrister John Kelly, Lindholm had "lost everything." Unemployed and living out of her car, she decided her only option was to kill Amey – a man she'd once hoped to start a family with.

"Her sense of grievance at the situation she found herself in needs to be viewed through that prism," Kelly told the Supreme Court following Lindholm's plea of guilt. "She had lost all sense of proportion at that stage. But she blamed Amey for the straights she was in because … she says she had the most wonderful upbringing and childhood she could hope to have."

Kelly added that by 2013, Lindholm was a "40-year-old woman with no prospect that she could see, no means of support, and no property or assets to her name," but added that none of this information "ameliorates what then happened to Amey."

Despite her desire to see Amey killed, Lindholm knew wouldn't be able to commit the murder on her own. If she wanted her ex-lover dead, she'd need to convince her new lover to do the dirty work. While Lindholm considered her relationship with Trabert to be nothing more than a "fling," he had fallen "madly in love."

"Trabert was infatuated with her," said Chief Crown Prosecutor Gavin Silbert QC, noting that the pair were involved in an "intense sexual relationship." He added that Trabert had even left his wife and children to move in with Lindholm – but there was a price to be paid.

"He couldn't keep his hands off her, and the return for her affection was that he kill Wayne Amey," Silbert said. "It was only with the seduction of Travert that she achieved her aims."

According to Silbert, Trabert wasn't Lindholm's first choice. In fact, he told the Victorian Supreme Court during Lindholm's trial that the stripper had attempted to convince several other former lovers to help her get rid of Amey, but Trabert was the first one to agree to her plan.

However, Trabert did need a bit of persuading. Silbert told the court that Lindholm used her sexuality to seduce Trabert into doing her bidding – to the point where, Silbert said, Trabert was completely obsessed with her. Even while locked in a remand cell following his arrest, Trabert sent flowery love notes to "darling" Lindholm.

"I'm missing you so much that I can't sleep because you are not with me ... we are so good together," one note read. "I can't think of my life without. All my love, Toots."

Trabert ended his note with a carefully drawn heart containing the words "I love you forever."

According to plan

The murder was carried out on December 10, 2013 – the day before Amey and Lindholm were due in court to resolve their dispute over a $1.1 million rural property they owned in Bittern. Lindholm directed Trabert and his accomplice, John Anthony Ryan, to attack Amey at his apartment.

The two men beat him repeatedly with a baseball bat, stabbed him, and choked him – and then wrapped him up and stuffed him in the trunk of the car. The group then drove to a remote farm in Mt Korong in Central Victoria, to get rid of Amey's body.

According to court reports, Trabert had tried to find a fourth person to help the trio "finish off" Amey, but this person refused to get involved. At this point, records state, Amey could be heard "begging for his life" from the trunk of the car. When the car was parked at the farm, Trabert and Ryan completed the murder.

"Post-mortem examination revealed that Amey had multiple stab injuries to his chest, fractured ribs, pallor and furrow to the left side of his neck in association with a rope, and multiple lacerations to his scalp," the court records revealed. "The opinion of the forensic pathologist was that Amey's death was a result of one or more of these injuries."

Lindholm kept a watchful eye on her suitor as he and Ryan pushed the body into a crevice between two rocks, ordering them to use more rocks and sticks to cover Amey's corpse and ensure it wouldn't be discovered.

Once the body was sufficiently hidden, Lindholm and Trabert had sex in the bushes, while Ryan went to a nearby Inglewood hotel to meet them for drinks. The trio attempted to use Amey's bank cards to clean out his accounts, and eventually set his vehicle on fire to destroy any remaining evidence.

"(Lindholm) was laughing and carrying on like it was nothing," Ryan told police. "She's on top of the world. They just wanted to f—-ing party, and I just felt ill, ill the whole way."

Charges laid

Lindholm, Trabert, and Ryan were all apprehended by police just days after Amey's murder. A car pursuit between Trabert, Lindholm, and police ended on foot – Trabert was nabbed by police, while Lindholm attempted evade them by crossing a creek. Ryan, meanwhile, was apprehended at a residential address in Coburg after the body was discovered.

"We have found Amey on the top of a hill," said Sen-Constable Philip Gynther, leading homicide detective on the case. "His remains have been place at the bottom of a crevasse between two large rocks. It's been a very long process ... the terrain all looks very similar."

According to court documents, Lindholm pleaded guilty to Amey's murder, while Trabert and Ryan plead their innocence – "each maintaining that it was the other who had killed Amey."

All three received sentences from Supreme Court Justice Lex Lasry – 25 years for Lindholm, 28 years for Trabert, and 31 years for Ryan. According to Lasry, Lindholm had shown "no remorse" for her role in Amey's murder – saying she "no doubt" felt ashamed and embarrassed, but he didn't believe she had a genuine regret for her "bizarre actions" in the "appalling crime."

Lasry also stated the trio had a history of "excessive use" of crystal meth – a drug which tends to fuel "extraordinarily violent criminal behaviour," he said.

While appeals were submitted for reduced terms, Senior Crown prosecutor Douglas Trapnell, QC, said each member of the trio was "equally responsible" for their roles in Amey's murder – whether as an instigator or as a physical killer.

"Because this was a pre-meditated plan and callous killing on the eve of a court hearing, where Amey was to exercise his legal rights, brings it very close to the worst case," Trapnell said. "This man was beaten in the basement of his apartment building where he had the right to feel safe. He was hog-tied ... then put in (a car) boot and remained alive for quite some time, albeit with (injuries including) fractured ribs."

Trapnell also argued that the trio had "desecrated" Amey's body by stuffing it into the crevice on Mt Korong, where, without the assistance of Trabert, it might never have been located. Following his apprehension, Trabert had led police to the farm where Amey's body had been hidden.

"The location of the body by my client allowed the family to seek some closure in having the body returned and afforded a proper burial," said Trabert's lawyer, Adam Chernok. "It's arguable it would have been a much more difficult case to prove and indeed may not have obtained the plea of Lindholm."

Chernok added that while Lindholm had a "primary motive" to kill her lover, his client's only motive was "put very simply, your honour, sex."

"If the killing of Amey is Lindholm's wicked design, it is not a truly shared motive in terms of the killing as I've described," Chernok said. "My client is motivated by sex in the context of his particular circumstances."

David Hallowes, who defended Ryan, claimed his client didn't become involved in the plot until after he'd been told that Amey was "mistreating" Lindholm. According to Hallowes, Ryan had believed the plan was only to "beat" Amey – and that without Lindholm's participation, the murder would never have happened.

However, according to Justice Philip Priest, the two men had ample opportunity to back out of the plan while Amey was still alive in the trunk of the car. The fact that they continued with the murder shows "how nasty this killing was."

"Lindholm sought to bring about Amey's murder for two years," stated the judgment from the Court of Appeal in October of 2016, dismissing the bid from the trio. "She tried to persuade others to kill him for her, and eventually, she persuaded Trabert to do it. Trabert and Ryan callously, ruthlessly, and violently carried out her wishes."

In fact, the statement added that Lindholm had continued to arrange for Amey's murder even after she'd broken into his apartment and received a community corrections order. According to court records, Lindholm and others had conducted surveillance on Amey, and she'd broken into the apartment even though she had a swipe card that could have been used to gain entry.

Records show she had told an associate that she'd done this so that "if something happened in the future, it would look like she did not have access to the property."

"It is difficult to overstate Lindholm's moral culpability for this crime," the court said. "She pleaded guilty but the (sentencing) judge found that she was not remorseful. In our view, the sentence imposed on her was a merciful one in the circumstances."

More than sex on legs

Supporting the charges were a series of text messages exchanged between Lindholm and Amey in the weeks leading up to his murder, included as part of the police evidence against Lindholm.

"Look at that ring on your finger Rob," read one message from Amey to Lindholm. "The one I designed, had made and ask you to marry me with, AND I MEANT IT. What better chance could anyone get? You cheated on that ring and me. Remember that when it's on your finger next time you sleep with him."

"Wayne you wouldn't take me back. I tried for months," said one of Lindholm's texts to Amey. "After I recognized my mistakes you still rejected me. I was only good enough to f—k. That was all. When I f—-ked up I was in a bad place lonely and messed up. I know that hurt and I don't know why I did it but the last few months when I begged to come home and I wanted you more than anything you still rejected me continuously. And took everything away."

"I need to feel like I'm more than just sex on legs," she said. "There's Robyn here too not just Collette."

Another text from Amey stated that Lindholm had gotten herself "in this position from a LIFETIME of lies, deception, drug abuse, selfishness and hate."And in another message to Amey, Lindholm told him that if he made her life any more difficult than he already had, "you will regret it Wayne."

According to Lindholm, the couple had been drifting apart for years. By the time their relationship started, Lindholm was in her 30s – ready to get married and start a family. Amey, though, already had a son from a previous relationship and decided to get a vasectomy. According to Amey, the couple "couldn't afford" a child because of their outstanding debts.

By 2009, Lindholm was even more frustrated with her relationship with Amey. He'd promised to retire with her at the Bittern property following his 50th birthday – but that never happened.

"She anticipated that the pair of them would live out there and she would raise her horses out there and they would see out their twilight years together there," said Kelly, Lindholm's lawyer.

Officially, the pair split in 2011, but according to Lindholm, Amey continued to reach out to her for casual sex, right up until his death.

"He was very into that and whenever he got drunk or smashed he used to call me and that was right up until not long ago," Lindholm told police after Amey was killed. "We used to do a lot of threesomes and he used to get me to bring girls home a lot."

However, despite what Ryan had been told about Amey "mistreating" Lindholm, she told police their relationship had never been violent. In fact, she claimed Amey was "kind" to her.

"We loved each other, but we just grew apart," she said. "I would never let anyone hurt (Amey) because he's never hurt me. He was always good to me."

An average guy

According to Amey's teammates from the Camberwell Hockey Club, he was happy, friendly guy – who happened to get in with a "fast crowd." While he wasn't known for sharing many details about his personal life, he had broached the topic of his relationship with Lindholm about three week before he was killed.

Amey had felt as though a weight had been lifted from his shoulders, believing that his dispute with Lindholm over the Bittern property was coming to an end – it was finally on the market, and once the property sold, Amey would be able to get a brand-new start.

"He spoke openly about a breakup some time ago that had turned sour and threatening," said Dugald Jellie, a teammate from the hockey club. "(Amey) was caught in a drama he couldn't undo. He'd tried restraining orders. He wanted only to quit his ex-partner and her friends, sell his country retreat, then one day sell his gym and start anew."

As a youth, Amey had been a top-grade hockey player. As an adult, he'd taken to playing in Camberwell's veteran's squad and working with the club to help develop its younger players. Jellie was one of his hockey mates, who had traveled with Amey to a game in Geelong just a few weeks before he was murdered. He was deeply affected by the news of Amey's death.

"It frightens me to think of (Amey) being hurt and in such peril. It is awful to think of him being so vulnerable, so helpless, so in need of his friends when none of us were there," Jellie said. "I can't stop but think of the moment he was jumped, and of his fears, and how alone he must have felt."

Active investigation

While serving her 25-year sentence for arranging Amey's murder, Lindholm received a new set of charges in June 2016 – naming her responsible for the murder of George Teazis, back in 2005. Appearing before the Melbourne Magistrate's Court via video link from the notorious Dame Phyllis Frost Centre women's prison, Lindholm refused to enter a plea, or speak at all, other than to confirm her name to the magistrate.

In 2017, defence counsel will hold a committal hearing and plan to cross-examine more than 20 witnesses, which will determine if Lindholm will then stand trial.

Investigations are ongoing to determine the extent of Lindholm's possible involvement in the disappearance of Shari Davison, as well.

KILLER SEDUCTRESS

GARY RACE

Shayna Hubers

Shayna Hubers is a 21-year-old graduate from Lexington, Kentucky. She grew up in a comfortably middle-class family and was a smart young woman. She graduated from Paul Laurence Dunbar High School in 2009, and went on to college. During high school, Shayna's friends described her as quiet and "most likely to succeed". Shayna graduated from Kentucky's prestigious School of the Arts after making Dean's list in 2012. She was in the process of pursuing a Master's Degree in counseling from Eastern Kentucky University when she took the life of her on-again off-again boyfriend, Ryan Poston and effectively put her life on hold.

Poston was a 29-year-old lawyer and business owner from a successful family of attorneys and executives. He was loved by his friends and family and admired by women. He was known to be friendly, respectful and respectable, and an overall good guy. He met Hubers in 2011 through mutual friends on Facebook and the attraction was instantaneous, as the first photos of Hubers that Poston saw were racy in nature. The two began to chat, and started officially dating shortly after they went on their first date. They continued their relationship for over a year. If it hadn't been for Facebook, the two more than likely never would have met, as Shayna lived 80 miles away from Ryan and had no reason to venture into Ryan's neck of the woods.

Throughout the entirety of the relationship, the couple sent thousands of text messages, including a conversation about possibly taking a two-week long break from each other and the relationship. Hubers was also known to post pictures of herself and Poston on Instagram. The seemingly happy couple exchanged over a thousand photo messages, as well as 20,000 messages through Facebook. Most of the Facebook messages had been sent by Hubers to Poston, who had responded to only a handful of them.

To people who weren't aware of the couple's dynamics, it appeared as if they were a happy couple who had everything going for them. They were both beautiful, successful, and driven. It was a match made in heaven- or so it appeared to be, but the truth was much darker and would become the subject of a complicated trial and a life term in prison.

On October 11, 2012, Hubers and Poston and his family had dinner at the young lawyer's home. After dinner, Hubers went home- she returned a few hours later, however, and the couple got into a heated argument. Poston informed his girlfriend that he wanted to end their 18-month long relationship, and it set Hubers off into a fit of anger. Her anger worsened when she was later told that Poston already had a date lined up with the 2012 Miss Ohio, Audrey Bolte. It's believed that the news of Ryan's new date was what pushed Hubers over the edge.

In the morning, Hubers' mother drove two hours to pick up her daughter and the two went out shopping. They were out for most of the day before Shayna was dropped back off at Ryan's house, telling her mother that she wanted to stay with him. Despite her other asking her numerous times to come home with her, Hubers was adamant that she wanted to stay at Poston's house. Shortly after, Poston became aware that Shayna was planning to stay at his place- he used this time to inform her that he had another date and didn't intend to spend the night with her. By 9 o'clock that night, the young lawyer was dead on his dining room floor.

At 8:53 that chilly Friday night, Hubers placed a 911 call from Poston's condo and said to the responding dispatcher: "Ma'am, I have...I have...I have killed my boyfriend in self-defense".

The dispatcher then asked what happened, to which Hubers replied "He beat me and tried to carry me out of the house and I came back in to get my stuff. He was right in front of me and reached down to grab the gun. I grabbed it out of his hands and pulled the trigger".

The dispatcher then instructed Hubers to step outside with her hands in front of her. Hubers complied, and responding officer, David Fornash's partner cuffed and took her away while Fornash himself went to investigate the crime scene.

Fornash and the other officers who responded to the scene, found Ryan Poston lying on his dining room floor next to a Sig Sauer .380-caliber pistol. The pistol, upon further inspection, was found to have belonged to Poston, who had a passion for guns. "...he would have them in his boot, he would have them in his holster..." says Poston's ex-girlfriend, Lauren Whorley, who claimed that Poston's love of guns made her feel safe.

Fornash went room to room, double checking that there were no other hiding in the apartment and upon finding Poston's body, officers found that he had been shot once in the back, twice in the head, and three times in his upper body. The coroner is called and Fornash sets off for the station where Hubers had been escorted into an interrogation room and sat waiting.

Meanwhile Poston, lying dead on his kitchen floor, was supposed to meet with Audrey Bolte at the Milford Inn bar for a night of drinks and harmless flirting. Poston, however, did not show up and Bolte went home feeling confused. When asked how she felt about him not showing up, Bolte said that it was odd for Poston not to show up or give some sort of notice that he wasn't coming, as he was a very responsible individual.

Friends of Poston claim that he and Hubers were never really in a committed relationship, as Poston lost interest in Hubers rather quickly and made several halfhearted attempts to break it off with her. In fact, by October of 2012, Ryan had made 3 attempts to sever Shayna's ties to him. According to text messages between Poston and his cousin, he was emotionally drained from dealing with Shayna. "I received 75 text messages from her. I am emotionally and mentally spent. I hope she leaves me alone" reads one message between the cousins. Despite this, Poston continued to go out with Hubers and pose for photos.

Shayna, confiding in a friend through text messages, said that Poston had told her that he's only with her because he felt bad when she cries. She is also quoted as saying: "My love has turned to hate."

In one particularly chilling message Shayna claims that "...tonight when I go to the shooting range with Ryan, I want to turn around, shoot, and kill him, and play like it's an accident." The next day, Shayna posts a photo of herself with a gun at the shooting range.

The night of the murder, Shayna was interviewed about the incident. Left alone in the interogation room, Shayne almost seemed proud of what she had done, reports Chief Bill Birkenhauer. He watched her on live camera snapping her fingers, dancing around, and muttering to herself "I killed him, I killed him."

Legally, officers were not allowed to interrogate her without an attorney present, so when she was brought into the interview room they didn't ask any questions. In fact, officers didn't say anything. Shayna, however, readily volunteered her story of how the events took place. She was rambling on for two hours before running out of things to say. According to officers, the men and women who took turns sitting with Shayna, quickly grew tired of her rambling and would have preferred to leave. "Shayna appeared to be nervous, or trying to cover something up" one officer said. "...her stories, after a while, stopped matching up and kept changing." This, according to the officer, might have been happening as a result of Shayna realizing that she was in over her head.

When speaking about Poston's death, Hubers said that she knew he was dead because he was twitching. Her exact words were: "Literally, that's when I knew that he was dead or close to it...the twitching...and that was it." She goes on to explain how she couldn't let him sit there and twitch. She couldn't stand to sit there and watch him die so she shot 5 more rounds into his body to finish him off.

In addition to building a case of self-defense and trying to convince officers that she deeply loved Ryan, she claims that "he was very vain...he wants to get a nose job...I shot him right here-" she pointed to her nose and continued her story "...and I gave him the nose job that he wanted."

Officers didn't buy Shayna's claims of self defense due to lack of evidence that Poston was ever abusive towards her. "She claimed that she was pushed and that he hit her, however, there were no visible marks or wounds at all on any part of Shayna's body" says former FBI profiler James Fitzgerald.

"There was no evidence in Ryan's condo that there was a fight" adds Laura Richards, a prominent criminal behavioral analyst.

Photos from the crime scene show evidence against Shayna's claims of a fight, as there were a number of pill bottles and bullets standing on end on the table. Had a fight taken place, they would have been knocked over or displaced and the murder area would have been left a mess. Instead, it was neat and tidy other than the pool of Ryan's blood that was left behind after the shooting. Shayna had also claimed that Poston had thrown her against a bookshelf. The bookshelf in question, when police arrived, was undisturbed.

As for Shayna's odd behavior when left alone, Richards believes that it was an act in an attempt to appear mentally unstable and open the door for the insanity plea should her self-defense claims fall short. "She couldn't decide which plea to go with- self-defense or insanity. So, she decided to open the doors to both and see which one panned out the best."

After three hours of deliberation, Shayna is charged with one count of first degree murder. In 2014, her trial is well underway and a forensic pathologist mentions that at the time he was shot, Poston had been sitting down- a fact that goes against what Shayna had said previously. According to Richards, this fact alone blows Shayna's claims of self-defense out the window as it shows that Ryan was not charging at her in a fit of rage, as she had previously claimed. Instead, he had been seated and had been seated great distance away from Shayna at the time of the murder. Forensic expert Howard Ryan backs this theory up by going into detail about the shots that Shayna fired at Poston. He says that the first shot was to Poston's head, a fact that is significant due to the lack of blood found on Ryan's shirt.

"If he had been standing up, the gravity would have brought it down...straight down the shirt through the bottom to the pants" he says.

Using the blood stains on the table, Ryan is able to provide further detail as to why he believes that Poston was sitting down. "When she shoots him in the forehead, his head goes down on the table." Poston's head would not have fallen onto the table if he had been in an upright position. From here, Ryan suspects that Poston's back was left exposed, setting him up for the next shot. At the same time that he is being shot a second time, his right arms falls limp and opens up the area of his body that will receive the third shot- which is right underneath of his arm. After this, his body slumps to the floor and remains there until it is removed by the coroner.

Three of Shayna's cellmates testified against her that day, claiming that she had told them that she intended to kill Ryan that night and that he had never been abusive to her. "She laughed about shooting him in the face and giving him the nose job he always wanted" claims Cecily Miller.

Another inmate, Holly Nivens, claims that Shayna made the whole abuse story up. When speaking about the bruises and scratches that Shayna would show people, Nivens claimed that Shayna inflicted them on herself.

Shayna also told her cellmates that she had messed the apartment up and thrown objects around to make it appear as though a vicious fight had taken place.

Shayna didn't take the stand, but prosecutors used her social media and interview footage as a substitution. Despite the overwhelming evidence against Hubers, her defense team maintained its argument that Poston had been abusive and that Shayna had acted out of self defense when she shot him.

A toxicologist was asked to plead in Shayna's defense and said that at the time of his death, Ryan had a strong mix of Xanax and Adderall in his system. He argues that these medications could have caused outbursts of anger and violence, making it possible for Ryan to snap and come after Hubers with a both his fists and then later on, a deadly weapon such as a gun.

A clinical psychologist was also called to testify on her behalf, and he diagnosed her with bipolar disorder with narcissistic tenancies, and post traumatic stress disorder (PTSD).

"She was very distraught. She was depressed" says the psychologist who claims that Shayna had told him that she had suffered from sexual abuse as a child, and was recognized as having alcohol and prescription drug abuse issues.

On the day of the trial, Shayna painted herself as a model girl friend to Poston, claiming that he had been going through a lot and that she had always been there for moral support.

"I was always good to him" she said.

Again, the jury didn't buy the story. Five hours after her trial started, Shayna was officially charged. She appeared back in court three months later for sentencing and was given 40 years behind bars. Shayna's defense team tried to lower the time before she becomes eligible for parole to 8 years instead of 20, but was denied this motion.

Just six months later, her legal team filed another motion seeking a new trial. According to her team, one of the jurors who convicted Shayna had not been legally eligible to convict her as he was a convicted felon himself. This, according to Kentucky law, made him unable to serve the court and gave Shayna's legal team a reason for a new trial.

It's said that Shayna's new trial date is set for early 2018. Until then, she is behind bars and serving her 40 year sentence as planned.

The new trial was originally set for January of 2018, but has been put on hold for 4 months longer at the request of Shayna's legal team. The extra time, according to her attorney, will be used to prepare.

Despite the 40 year sentence, Ryan's friends and loved ones are left with a sour taste in their mouths. Lauren Whorley, in an interview with a news station, claims that she wishes she would have known what was going on- maybe then she would have been able to help and prevent Ryan from getting too tangled up in Hubers. She also said that she believes the trial should have been handled in an "an eye for an eye" fashion, meaning that what Shayna did to Ryan, should have been done back to her as justice.

"Maybe it's traditional, old-school mentality, but if you kill someone, then you know, it's an eye for an eye. And what you due unto others should be done unto you" she said.

For her, however, the sentencing brought a sliver of much appreciated peace. "I was there when they read it" she said about the final verdict "It was the longest 30 seconds of my life."

Matt Herren, a close friend of Ryan, still struggles to make sense of what went wrong that night. "I think about him everyday," he says "You just don't think something like that will happen to someone you know."

Like Whorley, Matt wonders if there is something he could have done to prevent Ryan from suffering the fate he did. "I know a lot of people in his life feel the same way" he says to "48 Hours" correspondent Peter Van Sant.

Van Sant asked Herren what was lost when Ryan was killed and Herren responded with "He's the type of person you want in your life. Not just a friend, but a loving son, a protective, older brother. He had three younger sisters that he adored." Poston had cared deeply for his three younger sisters and only ever wanted the best for them. In return, they showered him with love and looked up to their older brother.

Ryan and his family had been close-knit, despite his mom and dad divorcing when he was a child. He was close to his father, and when his mother remarried, he grew an attachment to his new step-father, Peter Carter. Ryan thought of him as a second father.

According to Sarah Robinson, a woman who had grown up with Shayna, her future had seemed promising as well. Shayna had been a good student and was never in any trouble.

"I thought she was, close to genius, in my opinion" she said " I mean, she was always in AP classes. Always getting A's in everything."

During her academic career, Hubers had received various awards for academic excellence and leadership.

"She liked to succeed at anything and everything she did" Robinson concludes.

When Van Sant asked her what Shayna had been like with boys in high school, Robinson mentioned that Shayna could be dramatic. "If a guy, broke up with her or something, she would take it pretty hard" she explained "...crying, and a maybe a bit of screaming..she didn't really like to let things go."

When asked if Shayna had been happy with Ryan, Robinson said that as far as she knew, she had been. As far as she knew, they had both been happy.

Ryan's friend, Allie Wagner, claimed that there was something wrong with the relationship from the start when she was asked the same question about Ryan. According to Wagner, Shayna had been cold upon their first meeting. "You could just immediately tell that...that she was obsessed with him," she says.

"He was busy with work..he didn't really have time for anyone" Herren adds. "He didn't want to hurt her feelings..that wasn't the kind of person he was."

As Shayna's denial towards Ryan's disinterest progressed, he started to wonder if he might need to put a restraining order out against her. "This is getting to be restraining order level crazy..." he wrote in a text message to his cousin "She's shown up at my condo 3 times and refuses to leave each time."

Ryan's neighbor, Nikki Carnes claims that there may have been two sides to the tumultuous relationship. She says that Ryan may have been emotionally abusive. According to Carnes, Shayna complained frequently of Ryan putting her down. "She told me that he would say she needed a boob job or a face lift and that she was fat and needed to lose some weight" she says.

Van Sant then asked her why Shayna wouldn't have left and she replied "I guess because she was young and she always told me she loved him." Carnes also told Van Sant that Shayna did everything for Ryan from taking his dog outside to picking up and doing his laundry. On the night of the shooting, she also reportedly heard gunshots but didn't hear the couple fighting, as Shayna had claimed that they had.

Wagner, when asked what she thought could have happened that night replied, "I think she went over there...tried to talk him out of breaking up with her. And I think he just stood his ground for the first time," she said "I think he just said no, like, this isn't working. So she picked up the gun and shot him."

Chief Birkenhauer agreed with Wagner's theory "He wanted to break up with her...I think that Shayna was not gonna be broken up with" he said in an interview with Van Sant.

Prosecutor Michelle Snodgrass explains why Shayna's pleas of abuse were dismissed. "Someone who is in shock does not pirouette," she says in response to the police videos of Shayna singing and dancing in the interview room "Within hours of putting six bullets in Ryan Poston and watching him die, she was dancing and singing."

"There were hundreds of thousands of text messages. And most of them were from Shayna. For every 1 message Ryan sent, she sent probably 50," Snodgrass says "She couldn't stop herself."

According to Snodgrass, rejection was what ultimately pushed Shayna over the edge and drove her to kill the man she so desperately loved.

"Ryan's a bright guy; he's a lawyer" says Van Sant to Snodgrass "Why wouldn't he get a restraining order?"

"Under the law in Kentucky, he didn't qualify for a restraining order. The law in Kentucky required the two to have been living together or to have been married" she replied.

Van Sant then spoke to Hubers' mother, Sharon, about the tragedy. "She graduated cum laude in three years at the University of Kentucky. She was pursuing a Master's Degree in school guidance counseling," she said.

"And what do you want people to know after reading this" Van Sant asked "...in relation to this case?"

"Shayna Hubers is not a child, a girl, a person that would murder someone; that would wake up and say 'OK, I'm going to shoot somebody"

"I want the world to know who Shayna is. And I want them to hear it from her mother" she concludes tearfully.

Hubers and her mother had been close most of Shayna's life, according to Sarah Robinson. "I think she was very close to her mom. I think her mom, for a good portion of her life, could have been her best friend."

This statement is backed up by a quote from Sharon Hubers in her interview with Van Sant: "That child has been a blessing to me. She's my whole life."

"The word that has been used to describe your daughter is evil" Van Sant teold Sharon.

"She's far from evil. Shayna has a heart of gold. She's like her mommy...a loving spirit. That's what I want the world to know" she replied.

After the trial, Shayna spoke up for the first time. Despite having killed their beloved family member, she didn't apologize to Poston's family. Instead, she apologized to her family and friends, and speaks only of herself.

"I'm sorry to my family. And I'm sorry to my friends for letting them down. And I'm sorry for the money my parents had to spend on attorneys" she says, after being convicted of the murder.

"I do wanna help people. I do wanna be something better. And I do want to continue to grow and learn" she said to the judge "And I just don't think a 40 year sentence will help me. I don't think it would benefit me any."

Judge Fred Stine replied to Shayna's statement with his own choice words. "What I think happened in that apartment was little more than cold-blooded murder."

Regardless of what happened that night, a promising young lawyer lays dead, and a successful college student sits rotting behind bars. Two families have been destroyed, and law officials are left baffled. Both the victim and offender have been robbed of their lives- and for what? For a reason that the offender calls love.

Killer Seductress : Pamela Smart

Sarah Thompson

The case of Pamela Smart is infamous and retold in popular media through episodes on crime-based drama. What is it about Pamela Smart and her affair with a fifteen-year-old boy that draws society to continue to retell her case? The murder of Gregory Smart, Pamela's husband, is one that tells a story not often seen in the trends of women who commit murder.

Women who kill are so statistically and socially interesting to us that we, as a society, often gather up their specific stories into anthologies and special documentaries. Television shows like "Snapped" and "Deadly Women" focus exclusively on female cases of murder. Meanwhile, television shows that have been going on since the early nineties, like "Forensics Files", have an overwhelming number of male offenders. Of course, this isn't to say that women are incapable of murder, or that they do so infrequently. In fact, statistics have proved that women are entirely capable of killing, and often do so.

Information gathered by the Bureau of Justice Statistics, with data gathered between 1976 and 1997, shows the rate of murder committed by females was about 1.3 per 100,000. That is to say, for every 77,000 women, one would end up to be a murderer. The victims, in this case, were overwhelmingly the spouse. 60,000 murders were committed by women between the years of 1976 and 1997, and 60% of the victims were an intimate partner or family member.

While these numbers may be shocking, the context of the killings is also important. For example, 92% of all women in California prisons are estimated to have been battered or abused by either the spouse, intimate partner, or family member at some point in their lives. In 1992, data gathered by the Georgia Department of Corrections showed that of the 235 women that were currently serving time for either murder or manslaughter, 44% of those women had killed either their husband or intimate partner. However, of those women who had revealed that they had killed their spouse, 96% of them also admitted to having suffered domestic violence in the relationship.

Overwhelmingly, the reason that women kill is to escape a relationship with an abusive partner. With this knowledge, the next question is: what of the women who kill without the thought of self-defense in mind? What are the reasons and motives of the women who kill their perfectly loving and agreeable spouses? The women who kill in self-defense can be empathized with. But there is still a seedy underside to female murderers, the ones who manipulate the people around them and use others to their advantage to do away with their spouses. Not all women kill directly, after all. Some women manipulate others to do the deed for them.

The story of Pamela Ann Smart began in 1967. She was born as Pamela Wojas, on August 6th, in Coral Gables, Florida. A middle child, Pamela grew up as the second of three children. Her sister, Elizabeth, was six years her senior while her brother, John, was three years her junior. The children were born to a father who worked as a commercial airline pilot and a mother who was a part-time legal secretary. Her home life was good, and she went through childhood unmarred by violence or abuse by either her siblings or her parents. During her elementary school days, Pamela and her family moved from Florida to Windham, New Hampshire. There, Pamela flourished. She attended high school at Pinkerton Academy in Derry. She became a cheerleader, and her high school days floated by, still untouched by any particular violence or trauma. She was popular, and while she had a strained relationship with her father, she was very close to her mother.

After high school, Pamela decided to return to Florida for college. She attended the Florida State University and during her time there, Pamela worked on the radio, where she hosted a once a week show at WVFS. The show had a theme of heavy metal music, which Pamela loved. She called the show "Metal Madness", and her radio personality was under the alias of "Maiden of Metal". Pamela had a love for both heavy metal music and radio. After all, she was getting her degree in communications. Combining these two loves seemed like the only logical choice. It was during her time in college that Pamela met Gregory Smart. The year was 1986, and they were both at a New Year's Eve party. Pamela and Greg hit it off right away. Their relationship was intense from the beginning, and the two were seriously connected by February of 1987.

In 1988, Pamela graduated with honors and a degree in communications. Pamela was a smart and studious woman. Her academic achievements were nothing to be looked down upon. She achieved her degree in just over 3 years at the Florida State University, while maintaining a 3.85 grade point average. A year after her graduation, in 1989, Pamela and Gregory finally married, and Pamela went from Wojas to Smart. The marriage began as most marriages do, with a honeymoon phase that lasted only a short while. But while it lasted, the two were absolutely devoted to one another. They settled down in their hometown of Derry in New Hampshire, with a beautiful home on a quiet, residential street. Greg even bought Pamela a Shih Tzu, which she named 'Halen' after her favorite heavy metal group, Van Halen. Married young, Pamela was only 23 and Greg was absolutely devoted to her. They were the all American couple. Greg was excited about the start of his new life, with his perfect wife. His family recalls him talking at length about how Pamela would become a wonderful mother, so certain of his new wife's caretaking abilities.

Pamela, perhaps, was not as eager to begin life as a mother. She often described herself as a "typical Leo". That is to say, she always desired to be the center of attention. She had always been popular, even in high school, and she carried that bubbling charisma with her everywhere she went. While she was outgoing, loud and boisterous in her personality, Pamela was also needed to be in control: of herself and her surroundings, including the people in them. Her clothes were always nearly coordinated by color, and she lived by a very strict schedule that didn't allow much room for disruption. When her self-imposed schedule was thrown off, Pamela would become upset. Despite their fundamental differences, Pamela and Greg had a happy marriage - for a short time.

It was only 7 months into the marriage before the happiness the two shared started to waver. Their relationship went from blissful happiness to having serious issues. It's no surprise that the honeymoon phase of any relationship would begin to fade, but after only seven months Pamela and Greg's relationship was facing challenges. While Pamela longed to continue their rock and roll image, Greg began to grow up more quickly not long after their marriage. He cut his long blonde hair that Pamela had first fallen for, which was only the beginning of Greg's new, conservative attitude. He took up a job at the same company that his own father worked at. He traded in his intense love for heavy metal, which had first brought him and Pamela together, for the ambition that it took to become an accomplished salesman.

Pamela and Greg were simply growing apart as people, perhaps having married each other at too young of an age.

It was nearing their first year anniversary when Greg finally admitted to Pamela that he was having an affair. From then on, Pamela admitted, that her trust had been broken. She didn't feel important to her husband anymore. Her own interest in the marriage began to wane. After the admittance of the affair, Pamela's interests had turned into her career. After all, the graduated early with an astounding grade point average. Her desire to pursue a broadcasting career had not diminished in the slightest. Greg was unaware that Pamela wanted out of the marriage after the problem with the affair arose. Although she brought it up during every argument, talk of separation never came up.

Pamela, with her unhappy marriage and desire for freedom, took up a job at Winnacunnet High School in Hampton, New Hampshire, as a communications director. While it wasn't the glamorous job in broadcasting that she was hoping for, Pamela believed that it was a step in the right direction. Her duties included producing and distributing educational videos to the school districts. It wasn't quite the same as her heyday as the Metal Mistress back in college, but she was granted both her own secretary and student intern. In addition to this, Pamela also volunteered at the local drug awareness program, Project Self-Esteem, as an adult facilitator. She made a big impression on the freshman who were expected to participate in the program. All of the freshman students at Winnacunnet High School enjoyed Pamela - she was young, pretty and she could relate to them through a shared interested in heavy metal music.

Pamela got along well with the freshman who participated in the program. She was never patronizing and was young enough that she and the kids shared a lot of the same vernacular. She even wowed them with stories of her time in the heavy metal scene and her wild times backstage at concerts.

It was at Project Self Esteem that Pamela Smart met Billy Flynn. Their ill-fated meeting would change the course of both of their lives for good.

William "Billy" Flynn and Pamela Smart met in the fall of 1989. He was 15 years old, and one of the teenagers that worked on Project Self-Esteem. He was smitten with her right from the beginning, and would often go out of his way to help her. He even made routine visits to her office after the meetings. Billy Flynn shared Pamela's love for rock music. He was attractive and still growing into his looks, with blonde hair down to his shoulders - the same hairstyle that Pamela had loved in her own husband, and lamented it's lost. Despite his age, Pamela wasn't much older than most of the kids that she spent her days around, and it was easy for her to get lost in their acceptance. Around the same time that Pamela and Billy met, she was also reeling from her husband's admitted affair.

It was no surprise that Billy Flynn got caught up with Pamela. He was born just one day after an explosive argument between his parents and was always caught in the middle of their rocky relationship. He grew up watching his father mistreat his mother through anger and overbearing control. As the first child, it wasn't long until Billy was also the subject of his father's anger, and continued to experience it even after his siblings were born. Billy's father was reportedly a great man when things were going his way, but once that stopped his anger got the best of him and he would start yelling and berating whoever was within earshot. This put a strain on Billy and his relationship with his father.

Finally, spurred by his father having an affair, Billy's parents divorced. Soon after, Billy and his brothers moved with their mother from California to New Hampshire. It was here that Billy, young, angry, and suffering the trauma of a divorce, would meet Pamela, and change the course of his entire life.

Pamela's affair with Billy Flynn began when he was just 15. Pamela had become overly friendly with another one of the students under her charge, Cecelia Pierce, who was the student intern assigned to her at her position as a communications director. Pamela and Cecelia were like best friends, and Pamela showered her with attention. Because of their age differences, Pamela most likely made Cecelia feel important. After all, she was only 15 and Pamela was 23, an interesting adult who wanted to hang out with her and treated her like an intimate friend. Pamela's friendship with Cecelia soon began to show signs of being controlling, just as her "Leo" personality would suggest. The more time she spent with Pamela, the more her grades began to slip.

Pamela, Cecelia, and Billy would hang out like teenagers. While Gregory was out of the house, Pamela would invite the two teens over to watch movies or work on video projects together. It was during one of these times that Pamela and Billy first engaged in sexual intercourse. The time of the year was near the end of March, and Pamela had invited both Cecelia and Billy over to watch movies while her husband was out of state for a business meeting. After one of the movies ended, Cecelia went outside to walk Halen, the beloved Shih Tzu. While she was gone, Pamela brought Billy up to her bedroom, where she put on a piece of lingerie that she had bought specifically to seduce Billy Flynn. It was there, while their friend was out walking the dog, that the two had sex for the first time, in Pamela and Gregory's marriage bed.

Despite all the things she and the teenagers had in common, it's hard to understand why a grown woman would choose a 15-year-old as her lover - unless, of course, Pamela had other plans in mind for the needy and impressionable Billy Flynn. The morning after their first time together, Pamela said to Billy: "Last night was great, but we can't keep on like that." When Billy questioned why, Pamela said, "Because of Greg. If you want to keep seeing me, you'll have to get rid of my husband."

And just like that, the seed of Pamela's plan was planted. All that was left was to help it grow into a murderous, poisonous plant. Despite her conviction that they couldn't keep seeing one another, Pamela continued to engage in her relationship with Billy over the course of the next few weeks. Each time, she would continue to complain about the looming threat that her husband posed to their budding relationship. She even confided in Billy that Greg would beat her—although, this wasn't true. She continued to threaten that they couldn't keep seeing one another unless her husband was gone. Pamela explained to Billy that she couldn't get a divorce because her husband was too controlling. She told the young man that she would lose the condo and her dog. Billy, who had no reason to distrust his friend, teacher, and lover, believed the lies that she fed him. He was hopelessly in love, and it was then that the plans began to solidify.

Billy Flynn agreed with kill Pamela's husband. She had manipulated this outcome by repeatedly holding her affection and relationship hostage from him, with Gregory Smart as the threat that would tear them apart. Billy Flynn, just 15 years old and without the constitution of a murderer, flaked out on two attempts at Gregory's life. Each time, Pamela would berate him, threatening to leave him. While Billy couldn't yet see it, Pamela's motivations were clear: she was using her position of authority and her sexuality to manipulate Billy Flynn into committing the murder that she so desperately longed to commit, but refused to risk getting caught for. There was no star-crossed love between them, an angry husband keeping them apart. Pamela knew that she could manipulate a lonely, starry-eyed boy into disposing of her husband, and it wouldn't matter what happened to him after that.

Billy Flynn, faced with the threat of being left by the woman that he considered his lover, knew that he would have to start thinking seriously about killing Gregory Smart. He would later tell the jury that he thought Pamela would leave him if he chickened out of the murder one more time. Billy started confiding in his two friends, J.R and Pete, who had been in Billy's circle since he moved to New Hampshire from California. The three boys began plotting, with Pamela as encouragement. She gave them a deadline of May 1st, and promised the boys a cut of the insurance money that she would later collect.

While the boys were planning their attempt on Gregory's life, Pamela and her husband's marriage was falling into further disarray. Of course, this would be no surprise. After all, Gregory was living with a woman who was actively planning to kill him. There was no love left between them, and the strains of the marriage continued. They fought often and argued over the pettiest things. Gregory would come home to an empty house, and the couple would not see each other for days on end. Regardless of Pamela's desire to see him dead, the marriage was clearly ending. The two young lovers had simply grown apart. Where Gregory had grown into a businessman with responsibilities, Pamela had decided to stay surrounded by teenagers and relive her youth a while longer.

Finally, the plan to dispose of Gregory Smart was coming together. Unsurprising to anyone, it was Pamela who gave the boys primary directions. Pamela would leave her backdoor and cellar open. Billy, J.R, and Pete would enter the house and begin to tear it apart, making it look as if a robbery had taken place. She even instructed them to take electronics, jewelry and anything valuable to make it seem real. The lights were to stay off, as Pamela insisted that if her husband saw any of the lights on, he wouldn't come inside. She also didn't want the dog to be hurt, and so she instructed the boys to stick Halen in the basement so he wouldn't be traumatized by witnessing the murder of one of his owners. Finally, Pam insisted that they use a knife rather than a gun because she didn't want blood all over the apartment.

The plan would conclude with Pamela coming home to discover her husband, ostensibly murdered during a vicious robbery attempt.

May 1st, 1990, was the day that the plan would take place. That morning, Pamela got up and acted as if it were any other day and not the very last day of her husband's life. She exchanged morning pleasantries with her husband as they went about their morning routines. She tended to Halen and the two had breakfast together before they parted ways. Pamela must have been hyper aware of what was going on, and what would happen, while she watched her husband go about his day without any knowledge that it was his last. After all, most people never know which day is their last.

Gregory left for work before Pamela, who then headed out the door around 9:45 that morning. She had plans that would keep her busy all day and give her the alibi she needed to get away with conducting and orchestrating her husband's murder. She was attending a school board meeting that planned to go later than usual due to a salary review. Attending this meeting would ensure that Pamela wouldn't return home until after night had fallen - until Gregory was dead. Around 2:30 in the afternoon, Pamela and Billy met by his locker to discuss a small hiccup in their plan: they needed a ride to go pick up the getaway car, which belonged to J.R's grandmother. Perhaps leaving three teenage boys to do the dirty work is dispatching her husband wasn't the smartest idea that Pamela had, but it was all she had to work with. All the same, Pamela drove one of the boys out to get the car, and the rest of the plan was back in action.

Just before 8:30 pm, Billy, J.R, Pete and a fourth boy, named Raymond Fowler, commenced with the plan. Raymond was a boy often on the periphery of the group. His role in the plan was minor. Billy and Pete entered the condo while the other boys waited outside in the courtyard. While the ransacked the house, Billy tossed Halen into the basement - the dog, reportedly, fell down the stairs while the other boys laughed. After the dog was locked downstairs, they continued on with the plan that Pamela had set out for them. They took jewelry and took apart the electronics to make it look like a real robbery. After they had done their duty messing up the condo, Billy Flynn and Pete waited in the darkness for Gregory Smart to return home from his day, entirely unaware that they would be waiting for him.

Despite Pamela's insistence that they use a knife because of the mess, J.R had taken a gun from his father's collection and given it to Billy. The boys waited in the darkness by the backdoor, ready to jump Gregory the moment that he entered. When he did, it was Billy who leaped first, out of the darkness and onto Gregory. Pamela's husband was immediately overtaken by Billy and Pete. They stole his wedding ring to complete the robbery-gone-wrong image.

Finally, Billy said: "God forgive me," as he pulled the trigger just inches from Gregory Smart's head, and the man dropped dead to the floor.

The plan was completed. The boys escaped the condo, and their friends were waiting with the getaway car. They made their way back home. Billy had completed the task that Pamela had set out for him to do. He had killed her husband, in the anticipation that they would finally be able to be together. In the aftermath that followed, it was Pamela's job to play the grieving widow. According to the detective who worked on the case, Daniel Pelletier, she wasn't as good of an actress as she thought. Her interview with Detective Pelletier raised all kinds of concerns. Pelletier said, "From day one, she wasn't acting the grieving widow." Unfortunately, that was her only job in the plan she had concocted.

It was Pamela who insisted on an interview with the detective, and during that time Pelletier continued noticing strange things about her story. She described stepping over the body and noticing the speakers on the stand. She described the scene as a "botched robbery", rather than focusing on the death of her husband. The final thing that tipped Pelletier off, however, was when he took Pamela back to the condo to gather things she needed before closing it off as a crime scene: Pamela walked over the blood stain where her husband had died. Not around it: over it, multiple times until it was covered with a towel.

On May 2nd, just a day after the murder, detectives were already discussing the idea that it was Pamela who had done it, not yet aware of her influence on four teenage boys. It took two weeks before an anonymous tip led the detectives in the right direction: Cecelia Pierce. Detectives also got information from a boy named Ralph Welch, who had overheard J.R and Pete discussing their roles the homicide. While the detectives couldn't get the boys to talk, Cecelia finally told them everything. She agreed to be wired and tape a conversation between herself and Pamela in order to get the evidence that they needed. Pamela was convinced that it was her word against the boys and that she was home free, despite that word was getting around about her own involvement. It was Cecelia who managed to get Pamela's confession on tape, acknowledging that she knew that the murder was set to take place before it happened. That was all the police needed to set the rest of their plan into action to put Pamela away for good.

On August 1st, 1990, Pelletier arrested Pamela Smart for first-degree murder. Police Captain Jackson was on the scene as well, and had this to say of Pamela: "She thought she was smart, but she had no street smarts. [...] That was the problem. She that she was smarter than the whole world. But she made many mistakes, right and left."

The trial lasted only 14 days, and the main argument was about whether or not Pamela Smart had control of Billy Flynn and the other boys enough to make them murder her husband, or whether those boys did it on their own. Pamela continually insisted that she had no prior knowledge, and that she had lied to Cecelia on the tapes received of their phone calls. Pamela admitted to the affair with Billy Flynn, but refused to admit to prior knowledge of the planned murder. Her testimony consisted of confessions of love for the teenager. When it was Billy Flynn's turn to take the stand, he described everything: from Pamela's insistence that he kill her husband, to the night of the murder.

"I cocked the hammer back and pointed the gun at his head. I stood there for a hundred years, it seemed like," Billy Flynn said in his testimony. And while the court argued back and forth whether or not

Pamela had controlled Billy to do what he had done, it was clear why he had done it.

On March 22nd, 1991, the jury deliberated for all of 13 hours before they came back with a verdict: guilty. Pamela was sentenced to life without parole on the charge of accomplice to first-degree murder. A follow-up hearing sentences her with conspiracy to commit first-degree murder and witness tampering. New York State, where she still remains to this day serving her life sentence.

As for the boys, Billy Flynn and Pete are serving their time at the Maine State Prison in Warren, Maine. The fourth boy, Raymond Fowler, was paroled in 2003, sent back after violating the terms, but released again in 2005. J.R was given a 30-year sentence that was then reduced by 12 years to 18, and he was paroled in 2005. Cecelia Pierce, on the other hand, came out on top, having signed away the rights to her story of the case for $100,000.

Pamela Smart is an interesting case when it comes to women who kill. After all, she didn't lay a hand on her husband. However, she abused the influence that she had on her impressionable students and managed to use a combination of sex and power and to manipulate a young boy into committing a crime that he could never take back, and one that would never have crossed his mind had Pamela not been the one to put it there. So, despite the fact that she wasn't even in the house while her husband was killed, Pamela Smart still goes down in history as one of the most infamous "women who kill".

AMNESIAC KILLER : THE TRUE STORY OF DANIELLE STEWART

LES ACKERMAN

"I would punish all of those who had never lost anything, those who had never had anything taken away from them. I would let the anger from my chest reach out and explode in spectacular violence." - An excerpt from a poem by Danielle Stewart

Danielle Stewart had a normal and happy childhood until around the age of seven. Both of her parents were public servants and the family lived in the Curtin, Canberra region of Australia. She had one younger sister and the family seemed en route to living a normal, happy life.

Danielle was particularly close to her father during her childhood years. He took her swimming, read books to her at night and sang to her. She described him as being a man with a great sense of humor and the kind of man who "did all the things that dads do."

At the age of seven, however, Danielle's life took a traumatic turn. Her family was building a holiday house in the NSW south coast town of Batemans Bay. Danielle, unfortunately, came into the cross hairs of a sexual predator.

The man was a neighbor and Danielle would come over to his home to watch TV as they had no television of their own in their holiday house. The man was a married real estate agent in his 50s. He would let Danielle and a friend come with him to outings where they would examine unoccupied houses he was selling. It was there, inside these homes, that the assaults would take place.

Danielle would be under the man's spell for over three years before they molestations came to an end.

When she was eleven years old, tragedy struck again in the form of losing her mother to cancer. Distraught, her father sent her away for a weekend with a friend of a family. The family had a teenaged son, however, who constantly harassed Danielle, molesting her as well.

Her father would remarry six months later to a woman who had three children of her own. Danielle felt betrayed by her father's remarriage and tried to commit suicide with an overdose of pills. Her father himself had suffered from depression and fell apart emotionally after the death of Danielle's mother.

"I've always believed that depression and mental illness is inheritable," forensic psychologist Pauline Malloy said. "Sometimes through genetics, sometimes through thought processes. With Danielle, she clearly inherited some mental illness from her father's side of the family as her dad suffered from depression as well as her paternal grandfather."

Her maternal grandparents arrived and offered that Danielle come live with them. Danielle didn't want to go, she wanted to stay with her Dad but her father didn't want her screwing up the dynamics of his new family with her bad behavior.

He wanted her gone.

So Danielle was given two choices, either go live with her grandparents or go to a youth shelter.

Danielle chose to run away

"Danielle suffered numerous traumas, back to back," Malloy said. "The loss of her innocence, the loss of her mom and then the rejection of her father. Any of the above could have been cause for life altering psychological trauma but she suffered all of these within a four year time span. It had to crush her psychically and she did not have the life experience to cope."

Running away, the twelve year old girl roughed it out on the streets. Finally, she grew tired and returned home to her father. She would not be treated as the prodigal daughter, however, as her father had her bags packed and waiting. He drove Danielle to a local youth shelter and dropped her off.

Danielle would remain there for the next three months.

Danielle did not like the youth refuge. There was a lot of drug use, alcohol and she once again experienced sexual abuse.

"This was a horrid life for her at this point," Malloy said. "At some point I think she broke down psychologically and the seeds for future violent behavior were planted here."

RETURNING HOME

She eventually returned home to live with her father but he had settled in with his new family.

"I felt so alone, unloved, misunderstood," Danielle recalled. "and as the problems at home got worse, I got worse. I was sneaking out of the house, drinking, drugging. I missed my mum so terribly, I just wanted to be with her."

Danielle would attempt suicide on several occasions, leaving permanent scars on her wrist.

"I used a razor in my bedroom downstairs," Danielle said. "There was no internet back then and I didn't know how to do it [properly]."

On her 13th birthday, her father celebrated by throwing her out of the house once again. She would go and live with her friend Elle O'Brien and her mother. O'Brien's mother fed her and took her in, allowing the unwanted girl to remain there for four years.

At the age of sixteen, she enrolled at Narrabundah College and become a student of renowned poet Geoff Page.

"She was leagues ahead of anyone I've encountered writing contemporary poetry at that age," Page recalled. "She had some of the same virtues as Sylvia Plath, a real feeling for adventurous imagery. There was a lot going on in her brain at an intense level and she had the talent to turn it into something moving."

Under the guidance of her teacher, Danielle published an anthology of poems called "I for Icarus."

Danielle would go on to study performing arts at Melbourne's Monash University before traveling to Sydney to share an apartment with her step-sister, Myfanwy Thompson. Both young women would indulge in alcohol and prescription drugs, becoming the catalyst for each others self-destructive behavior. Myfanwy, however, would suffer a freak accident in falling off a cliff while taking ecstasy.

The loss devastated Danielle as she considered Myfanwy to be her best friend.

"Her boyfriend had got into dealing ecstasy," Danielle said. "I couldn't handle seeing her wasted all the time, so I'd moved out with other friends."

Her younger step-brother, Tristram would later die of an aneurysm after being diagnosed with schizophrenia.

MEANDERING THROUGH LIFE

Danielle was now 24 and wandered aimlessly through life. She went from one job to the next until she met the 50-year old Chaim Kimel in late 2000.

"They met on the dance floor and hit it off immediately," journalist Byron Kaye said.

Despite the age difference, Chaim Kamel was a stylish man with his own business.

"He was a bit of a bon vivant," crime author Paul Kidd said. "Lived in the good part of Sydney. A good lifestyle."

"He was very charismatic, very gregarious, very charming, very generous, strong and creative," Danielle said. "He loved his children and they loved him."

Kimel had been a successful entrepreneur, dealing in antiques. She got a job working for Chaim in his furniture store, Eclectica in Mosman. Kimel had put Danielle in charge of bookkeeping.

The two got along exceptionally well, at first, with common interests in art, music, and food.

"Danielle was a very attractive," Kidd said. "Petite, blonde, loved to drink. He (Chaim) was an older man but a really good style of a bloke."

The relationship started platonic in the beginning.

"He made some advances which weren't initially reciprocated," Kaye said. "But over time, they became intimate and it was on."

Kimel thought Danielle was a "prize catch". He invited Danielle over to visit his family and she was impressed with how close and living they were. There she saw, for the first time since her early childhood, a loving family that she could be a part of.

Danielle moved in with Kimel who had the time lived with his ten year old son Jordan. He also had a daughter, Amber and Fred, who were in their early twenties and late teens respectively.

A CHANGE IN DEMEANOR?

One of her friends, however, thought that Danielle changed after she met Chaim. She described him as being very possessive and told her what to do.

"I loved him," Danielle said. "I still do. It is a love-hate thing and it won't ever go. With those types of personalities, there is that level of attention, you become their entire focus."

Danielle would have these kind of intense relationships all of her life and it seemed to be the fuel to her fire. She was irresistibly drawn to the drama and would have it on full blast with Chaim Kimel.

"Anyone who would have been in a relationship with Danielle Stewart would have been in a relationship that was doomed from the start," Kidd said. "The combination of psychological problems fueled by excesses of alcohol was always going to end in disaster."

COCAINE AND BOOZE

Danielle began substance abuse at an early age which only progressed as she got older. She now had a benefactor in Chaim as well as an enabler as he liked to party, indulging in cocaine himself.. He didn't realize, however, that the alcohol would only stoke the flames that would extinguish their relationship.

He also had a dark side, according to Danielle's grandmother. She described him as someone who was "demanding and overpowering."

"She (Danielle) went through life with a paranoia that people were going to leave her," Kidd said. "And she became very, very possessive of her partner and that fueled by alcohol was the basis of the majority of their problems."

CALL THE POLICE

Once the relationship turned intimate, things started getting out of hand. The two indulged in alcohol and had numerous fights in which the police were called in.

Danielle had been taking strong anti-depression medications and mixing these drugs with alcohol. One fight had gotten so severe that she took a restraining order out against Kimel.

On one occasion, Kimel violated the order and was jailed for one night.

"I'd moved into temporary accommodation and Chaim came after me," Danielle said. "He broke into my room and stole my laptop and wallet. The police busted him on the way out and took him to jail for the night."

Kimel explained to the police that he violated the order because Danielle had called him stating that she had swallowed fourteen Valiums.

"I'm fine when I'm not in an emotional situation," Danielle said, "but when I'm under threat, the flashbacks can be extreme."

"She (Danielle) had a borderline personality disorder," Malloy said. "When things go bad with her, they go real bad. That was how she lived her entire life up until that point. She had to engage in fights, drinking, drugs. Drama, drama, drama. If it isn't there, she will create it."

A PROPENSITY FOR VIOLENCE

Kimel's son, Jordan, was ten years old when his father first met Danielle. He recalled Danielle as a destructive psychotic stating that she would "cut up $10,000 worth of business suits, delete important documents from my father's computer. Once, she punched through a glass bathroom window and slashed her wrists. And she'd punch my father, too."

"Unfortunately, this was the pattern that was set," Malloy set. "They would argue, fight and then get back together. When they would get back together things would be more passionate and clingy than before. 'Please, don't leave me,' that sort of thing. But then the cycle repeats itself and it has to be more extreme in order for the couple to get that same 'high.'"

The couple would remain together and make attempts to appear respectable. In 2004, Danielle enrolled at a nearby college to finish her degree while they both started an online catering company called Epicurean. The money to start the company was borrowed from Danielle's grandmother, a total of $30,000.

Later that year, the couple would journey to India where they would marry at the Taj Mahal.

Danielle would claim, however, that the money the borrowed for the business is what kept her in the marriage .

"Part of the reason I married Chaim was because I was worried about my grandparents' money," Danielle said. "If I left him, there'd be no legal recourse for me to get it back. He took it without shame; he never planned to pay it back."

"Typical of people with borderline personality disorders," Malloy said. "Is that they have to play the role of the victim. It is a head scratcher as to why Chaim would borrow thirty-grand when he had his own business. Maybe he thought he would be placating her somehow with them being in business together and having her feel as if she were a part of things. But clearly he didn't need anything more on his plate."

BOOMERANG BABY

Danielle would leave Kimel a total of seven times during their seven year relationship. She would confide in her grandmother and friend Elle, saying she was unhappy. Then he would call and they would get back together.

"It (their relationship) was very alcohol fueled," Kaye said. "Very hedonistic. A lot of violent arguments."

Danielle blamed her inability to stay away from Chaim on her lack of self-esteem.

"While he could be caring, it was undermined by his desire to keep me enslaved to him," Danielle said. "When I left him, he'd follow me and get me back. When your sense of self-esteem is so low and a learnt helplessness has set in, you don't feel able to support yourself. My friends had dropped off because they couldn't stand him. The only times I responded with violence were when I was trying to leave and he'd try to stop me. He'd hide my wallet, phone, computer, passport. Those times always ended with me being in hospital, not him. I never tried to kill him: I tried to kill myself."

WHO WAS ABUSING WHO?

It became apparent to Kimel's family, however, that he had married a woman prone to violent outbursts. Kimel told his daughter than Danielle had bitten him on his thumb and arm as as smashing his glasses.

He had his glasses broken so much that it had become a "running joke", according to his daughter Amber.

After arguments, Danielle would delete Kimel's emails and computer files. Kimel had became so enraged at her actions that he kicked her out of the house. Danielle would return, kicking out the timber door.

WELCOME TO THE PSYCH WARD

Danielle had overdosed on medication numerous times during the course of her marriage. She would inform doctors that Kimel was controlling and that she had "nothing to live for."

His daughter, Amber, however, expressed concern for her father's well being and wanted him to sever ties with Danielle.

"He told me he'd made a commitment to be there for her and loved her unconditionally," Amber said. "He was convinced unconditional love would cure her."

"Chaim was the rescuer," Malloy said. "He couldn't help himself. Danielle was the beautiful damsel in distress. They had passionate sex together, he knew about her past, and he couldn't be another man that brought more pain in her life. He didn't want that. He thought that through his own sincerity and love that he could somehow bring her to a place of healing. But he wasn't a professional. And that isn't what relationships are for."

A NEW MAN

In 2006, Danielle separated from Kimel and met Melbourne university professor Joeri Mol. She moved in with him and became pregnant by December of that year. Danielle wanted to go back to Sydney, however, and didn't want to raise the child with Mol as a single mother.

"She went out with somebody else," Kaye said. "He was seeing other people but they could not stop speaking. They remained extremely close. The new fellow (Mol) wants to settle down and start raising a family. Which incidentally was Danielle's greatest dream, which was to have a family. But she's still drawn to Chaim uncontrollably."

A week later, she called Kimel and the two met to discuss a reconciliation.

"He (Chaim) told her that either she as a termination," Kidd said. "Or there's no hope if them ever getting back together."

She complied with his request, her second abortion in six months (the first with Kimel) and she once again went into a depression.

"Danielle desperately wanted to experience the happiness that she had before her mother died," Malloy said. "She always told her grandmother, 'I just want have a normal life. I just want to have a normal life.' What she really wanted was that family again. So now she spends her life grasping at straws, going from this man to that man, and getting multiple abortions."

BURNING THE CANDLE AT BOTH ENDS

The couple moved back in together in 2007 but this time their break-up would be much more volatile.

And violent.

"It was short lived (their reconciliation)," Kidd said. "Now that they were back together. It was business as usual."

Business as usual was a lot of fighting and alcohol coupled with a flurry of activity to keep up with the bills.

Danielle returned to college and continued to run their catering business, The Epicurean. In order to make ends meet, however, she took a part time job at a Sydney ad agency.

She couldn't juggle all of these things at once, so she turned to cocaine and alcohol. Her friends described her as "withdrawn" and "unsettled" after meeting with her after the latest reconciliation.

Danielle began to feel the itch to run away again, telling friends she now just wanted to earn some money on her own and get away from Kimel for good.

"How the hell could this have worked to begin with?" Malloy said. "You've got a woman with some serious issues, abused by men, abandoned as a child and now she's an alcoholic with major depression. The pattern is set in their relationship. Break-up, get back together, fight some more. Rinse and repeat. This can only end badly. The question was, how bad?"

THE FATEFUL DINNER

"The old problems kept resurfacing," Kaye said. "They kept on with the dinner parties. Living the good life. And with this came Danielle's terrible response to alcohol access."

On August 23rd of 2007, Danielle went out with Kimel to have dinner at a restaurant called Pescador. They were described in a police statement by their friend, Angela Batley, to be in "good spirits."

"It is noted by others there that Danielle seemed a little drunker than usual," Kaye said. "Things got a little bit more testy and Danielle left and decided to walk home."

After dinner, Chaim went with his friends to Angela Batley's home. He would call Danielle from the home and she said that she would come and pick him up. Things took a turn for the strange when Danielle came over but drove back without Chaim who ended up walking home.

Batley was concerned about the tenseness of the situation and called Kimel to make sure he got home safe. Kimel told Batley that Danielle was working on the computer but was "drunk" and that he had to go.

Danielle arrived at their home before Kimel. She told the 16-year old Jordan that she "shouldn't have gone to Angela's house. I've had too much to drink."

Jordan stated that Danielle began playing loud music through the computer, dancing with a drink in her hand. When Kimel arrived, he told her to turn the music down before the neighbors start complaining. An argument ensued before Kimel turned off Danielle's music himself. The argument escalated, the topics being the loud music then escalating to the fact that Chaim would change the password on the computer, which was an ongoing issue in their relationship.

She started to physically attack him but Chaim easily evaded the rushes of the drunk Danielle. Then in the heat of the moment, she picked up one of Chaim's antique ornamental knives he had on display. Chaim came forward, ordering her to place the knife down, then she stuck it into his stomach.

Chaim fell to the ground and she stabbed him again.

"They were both yelling for about 15 minutes," stated Jordan. "All of a sudden, I could hear them in the corridor outside my room. It sounded like someone was being hit or punched and I heard my father say, 'Why are you being violent and attacking me?' They kept fighting and I heard Danielle fall to the floor and scream. Soon after this, I heard my father say in a tense voice, 'What are you doing? Are you crazy?' I heard my father scream three times. I saw [his] white shirt was covered in blood all up the left side from underneath his ribs towards the middle of his torso. Danielle was standing about two metres away and she had our antique knife in her hand."

Jordan saw his father struggling to get to the front door. He was covered in blood and Danielle was hysterical, holding up the knife.

"So the son runs out of his room," Kaye said. "He finds his father clutching his stomach where he's been stabbed twice. Covered in blood. Barely able to speak."

Jordan then thought about attacking Danielle himself.

"He picks up a golf club then thinks for a moment, that he might avenge his father," Kaye said. "It's actually Chaim himself who tells him don't do it. Lying there, sort of holding himself together. The son puts the golf club down and nurses his father while he lies there dying."

Kimel would be rushed to the hospital but die on the operating table at St. Vincent's Hospital, bleeding to death from the two stab wounds to his stomach.

"To the end of his life," Malloy said. "Kimel was protecting Danielle. When his son wanted revenge, he held him back."

Danielle was arrested but plead not guilty on the grounds of self defense. Her blood alcohol reading, however, was five times the legal driving limit.

"It was a stupid, pointless, uncontrolled lover's argument," Kaye said. "And one split second decision led to this terrible outcome."

Danielle maintained no recollection of the events, as she mixed the anti-psychotic drug Seroquel with alcohol. She awoke in a prison cell and called out for her husband, seeing her name on the board with the word 'Murder' written next to it.

"It was the worst moment of my life," Danielle recalled. "In one instant, my entire life had changed and Chaim's had ended."

"Something was going to happen that night," Malloy said. "Her mind was on edge. This may not have been pre-meditated but she knew what was going to happen when she picked up that knife. Remember, she didn't just slash at him as a warning. She thrust the knife into Chaim. Not once. But twice. There was an untapped rage there that came to the surface at the moment. It had been bubbling for a long, long time and unfortunately Chaim Kimel could not foresee how this would end."

THE AFTERMATH

Danielle made a recorded phone call to her father a few days after the killing.

"If I could swap Chaim with me right now, I would do it immediately," Danielle said. "There is no way I meant to kill him."

"Again, I don't think the murder was pre-planned," Malloy said. "But it did seem to be part of Danielle's destiny. What we see here in her killing of Chaim was a metaphor of her own trauma. She was abused by a man in his fifties, molested by him from the ages of seven through ten. She grows into a beautiful woman can choose just about whatever man she wants but instead she elects a man in his fifties, over twenty-five years her senior. That is no coincidence. She is repeating her trauma from the past. But this time she wants to control it. She wants to exorcise the demons of the past so all of those violent fights are trial runs until finally she reaches for that knife and stabs Chaim, metaphorically killing the molester of her past. Now her husband, who actually really loved her, is the victim of this cycle of abuse that has finally come full circle."

Her father agreed to post Danielle's bail but would not agree to the 24-hour surveillance condition attached to it. Her father abandoning her yet again, she turned to her friend Elle O'Brien's mother. She came to bail out Danielle and secured her release after nine months.

Danielle then went to live with her grandmother.

Facing twenty-five years in prison, Danielle would attempt suicide two more times, one of them involving an overdose of Seroquel.

"When I took that Seroquel, I went into psychosis," Danielle said. "It was an out-of-body experience where I thought the nurses were talking about me even though they weren't. I was watching myself from afar. It was crazy, crazy shit. I am sure that is what must have happened on the night Chaim died."

"The psych med plus alcohol defense has become a cliched defense for a lot of killers," Malloy said. "Danielle had done her research. She had studied scriptwriting in school. Everything she said and did had a rehearsed feel to it."

FROM MURDER TO MANSLAUGHTER

The murder charge had been downgraded to manslaughter as Danielle maintained she had no recollection of what happened. She did not remember any of the events of what happened that night not to mention taking the ornamental knife and stabbing her husband with it.

She did not take the stand, however.

"Danielle was charged with murder," Kaye said. "She wept throughout much of the trial. It was very clear that she regretted what she'd done and she wanted him back and she felt quite horrible."

Kimel's children, however, saw Danielle as an imposter the more they investigated the case. They found a synopsis of a play that Danielle had been working on. In the story, one of the characters had a secret desire to kill her older husband.

Fred Kimel, Chaim's oldest son, noted that the play contained details on "jail architecture, prisoner psychology, different cell classifications, prisoner attire, prison visiting hours and life sentences."

The Kimel family once enamored with Danielle, now saw her in a completely different light.

"It was a university assignment, a book I was writing," Danielle said. "I heard that somewhere men kill their partners because they want them to stay, whereas women kill their partners because they want to escape. I know why I was writing about prison: because I was imprisoned long before I was [actually] incarcerated."

SENTENCING

Danielle would be sentenced to six years in prison. She would serve only four.

"There's no doubt that jail saved me," Danielle said. "It prevented me from harming myself with alcohol and drugs. I wouldn't recommend it, though."

During the first nine months of her term, she had been housed in the mental health unit. She could not stop crying. But the prison assigned her to a job in the kitchen and she found her fellow inmates to be helpful.

"I managed to get a few of the heavies on side somehow and avoided the others where possible," Danielle said. "I learnt to assimilate, to hide the fact that I was pretty and educated. I adapted where I could. In jail, I lost everything that made me me: my family, dog, business, house, studies, friends, freedom, clothes, make-up, choices. All I had was myself, my mind and my heart. I learnt to spot evil from a mile away - and evil does exist, I've come face to face with it - but I could still love. This is how I got through jail. Yes, I learnt how to operate within the system, but I could still see beauty in people, and I tried to speak to that."

"Danielle was a well-spoken, educated young woman," Malloy said. "But why the hell would she plead not guilty? She did her research on prison culture beforehand so a cynic can argue that she got off very, very light for what she did. Call it misandry, call it getting the female pass, Danielle was able to get off light for a cold-blooded murderer. She used all of the things from her past to mitigate her own culpability. Sexual abuse, parental death and abandonment down to psych meds and alcohol. She combined those things to get sympathy from Chaim and later from the her jury of her crime."

Danielle walked out of prison on June 24th, 2010.

She is now focused on the prospect of moving to Spain and becoming a professional writer.

"I've paid for what has happened and I've done all I can to fix the issues within myself that contributed to Chaim's death," Danielle said. "I see both a psychiatrist and a psychologist, both of my own volition, nothing to do with parole directives. I don't drink. I don't take drugs. I take responsibility for my actions. I write when I can. I try to love my friends and family. I try to see beauty in the world and I'd like to hope, one day, that I can contribute to that beauty. Still, I love. I still love Chaim. I still love my father. In the end, love will be all I have."

SHE KILLED THE PREACHER

John Fontaine

The Case of Mary Winkler

Mary Winkler, at first appearances, would seem to be an altogether normal woman. So too did her family, with a husband who was a Church minister and three young children, girls aged just eight, six and one.

The family lived in Selmer, Tenn., a small town occupied by around 4,500 people, according to the 2015 census. The town is situated to the south west of the state. Not much has happened in Selmer; the most famous person to have been born there was Chad Harville, former pitcher for the Oakland A's, and for one year, the Red Sox. He achieved a 4-9 win-loss record over his career in the MLB.

Today, the most famous- or infamous- person to have come from Selmer is Mary Winkler. In 2006, Mary sparked a border-crossing manhunt, and a court case followed nationwide. She had killed her husband with a shot to the back from the family's shotgun. But it was the gripping, and at times bizarre, court case which gripped the attention of the nation.

Matthew dead, Mary and the family Missing

The date was March 6th, 2007. It was a Tuesday like any other. Mary and Matthew were at home all day together, although Matthew was due to give a sermon that evening.

It was actually members of Matthew's congregation who found his body that night. They had visited his home to check up on him after he had missed the service he was set to give; instead, they found him lying dead, having been shot in the back.

There was no sign of Mary or any of their children at the home, and as such, they were reported missing. The authorities quickly sent out an Amber Alert, since nobody had any idea what could have happened to them, or where they might be. Family and friends had no information to provide police on their whereabouts.

There was every chance that the family had been kidnapped or murdered, and their bodies disposed of elsewhere, although police could not identify a break in, and had no reason to believe that anything of value had been stolen.

It was only a day later that she was arrested in Alabama, having run from the family home with her young children. They were found 350 miles away from home, at Orange Beach, and in the back seat of the van was the family's shotgun. It was certainly suspicious; but what reason could Mary have possibly had for committing such a crime?

The Trial

In the build up to the case going to trial, public interest ramped up. Speculation had been rife about why Mary would have murdered her husband, a seemingly nice, well respected member of the local community. Perhaps either one of them had had an affair, and Matthew had been killed in a crime of passion. Or maybe he had been killed for an insurance claim?

As such, the press reported every step of the story as it came out during the hearing. The trial began when a Tennessee Bureau of Investigation Agent John Mehr read a statement that Mary had made very soon after her arrest. In it, Mary claimed that the couple had been arguing about their family finances, before Mary had shot her husband with their 12 gauge shotgun. She had said that the last thing she had wanted was to actually murder her husband, but she had been brandishing the gun in an effort to convince him to work through their problems, together. The argument had been ongoing throughout the day, and Mary had finally snapped, resorting to drastic measures to be able to convince him. She had never intended to kill him: she had said in the statement, 'I don't want this at all. I don't want any of this to be, at all.'

The statement continued on, and Mary claimed that they had argued often and argued fiercely. 'He had really been on me lately,' Mary had said, 'criticizing me for things- the way I walk, I eat, everything. It was just building up to a point. I was tired of it. I guess I got to a point and snapped.'

At first glance, it would seem that Mary had simply lost her composure, become angry, and killed her husband 'as the red mist had descended'. But after their initial statement, Mary's attorney indicated that there was much more that would come out about Matthew's behaviour when she testified which would help to explain her actions. Clearly, there were more problems with their marriage than the occasional, albeit fierce, argument.

Mary's Crime

The case for the prosecution wasted no time in painting Mary as a cold blooded killer, who left her husband to die without remorse. Admittedly, the plain facts of the case made Mary seem unbelievably guilty. The prosecution relied on several of these facts in their attempt to convince the jury of Mary's guilt for the charge of murder.

Mary had disconnected the phone immediately after she shot her husband, stopping him from being able to call the emergency services, or receive any calls that may have come in. This suggested that Mary had been in full control of her actions, not panicking, since it is unlikely that somebody in a state of anxiety would think to disconnect the phone.

The fact that Mary had attempted to flee to Orange Beach, Alabama, was also a key point for the prosecution. Immediately after Matthew's death, Mary had taken the family minivan to the beach, with her three children. Later on in her defence, Mary would claim that she ran because '[n]obody would believe me, and they'd take the girls away and put me away.' Certainly, in many murder cases, the fact that the defendant flees the scene is a certain indicator of guilt.

The family's daughter Patricia testified that she couldn't understand her mother's actions. All that she knew was that she had heard a 'big boom', and the sound of something heavy hitting the floor. She quickly ran to the bedroom to see her father on the floor, and her mother holding the shotgun. She had no idea what could possibly have provoked her mother to shoot him.

Another sticking point was that the family finances had been 'in shambles' just before the murder had taken place. This had led Mary to become embroiled in what is called a 'check kiting' scam. In it, she had received checks from unidentified accounts in Canada and Nigeria, and had ultimately fallen to a financial scam that had lost the family money. Prosecutors claimed that this could have somehow instigated the argument that led to Matthew's death, and that Mary had felt as if she had no way out of the scam.

They also jumped on the fact that in an initial conversation with investigators, Mary had told them that their marriage was a happy one, and that '[t]here's no poor me. I'm in control.' They clearly wanted to paint a picture of Mary as remorseless, deceitful, and smarter than she looked.

The Cross-examination

During her cross-examination in court, Mary stated that she didn't remember grabbing the gun from the closet in which it was kept. What she did remember was that 'something went off', 'hearing a loud boom', and that 'it wasn't as loud as I thought it would be.' She did admit that she had shot her husband. Matthew rolled from the bed- upon which he had been lying as they had argued- and dropped to the floor. Mary described smelling gunpowder.

Prosecutor Walter Freeland asked her whether she understood that 'pulling a trigger is what makes it go boom', to which she replied that she did.

Matthew asked her why she had snapped and shot him. She could only say 'I'm sorry.' The shotgun blast had been inflicted from behind, directly into Matthew's back, and had caused severe damage to his organs and spine. According to prosecutors, he had in fact still been alive as Mary had run from the house.

But these simple facts were far from the end of the story, as Mary was to reveal.

Appearances and Revelations

At first, Mary spoke of her husband not in the past tense, but in the present, as if she couldn't quite understand how final her actions really had been. In reminiscing about happier times, Mary told the court that her husband was an intelligent, social man, and that the family had shared many 'good times' together. She also seemed to enjoy talking about her children, and the happiness they brought her.

This happy family life, however, was simply one side of the marriage. Mary's attorney stated that '[w]hat went on behind their closed doors is going to have to be told ... Some of what we've got from the state of Tennessee touches on sexual abuse.' Their defence was that Matthew had made Mary's life a 'living hell': '[w]e will show you proof that he would destroy objects that she loved, he would isolate her from her family and he would abuse her not just verbally, not just emotional and not just physically—in other ways, too.'

Just before the murder, Mary claimed that Matthew had been threatening their children and even attempted to throttle their infant daughter, Breanna. He had been shouting, angry, because he had wanted a son. As the case went on, it became obvious that this was only the tip of the iceberg, however, and more and more sordid details of their home life would come to light.

Matthew, Mary claimed, was a violent, abusive husband. Shortly after their marriage, he ordered her to stop socialising with any of her family and friends (a common tactic among abusive spouses in order to further isolate their partners from potential help). Winkler's sisters described how Mary seemed stuck in her marriage, unhappy, but unable to leave. In an interview, they said that 'As the years went on, she seemed to be nervous to show love towards us.'

Mary was commonly 'screamed and hollered' at by her husband. 'He just flailed. He's a big guy and he was just all over ... He'd point his finger inches away from my nose. Whatever he was upset about, it was my fault,' Mary had said. It could be over anything: 'I was fat, my hair wasn't right, the girls, if something went wrong, it was my fault. I didn't know when it was coming.' Mary described her situation as one familiar to abused wives and husbands across America.

Her attorney, Steve Farese, provided further information based on his conversations with Mary. She had needed her husband's permission for everything, even for getting her hair cut. 'This was constant, and she lived a life where she walked on eggshells.' This abuse, he said, had given Mary symptoms of post traumatic stress disorder, simply because 'she didn't know what was going to happen next.' Furthermore, a psychologist testified as part of Mary's defence, saying that her symptoms were those of clinical depression and PTSD.

During her time on the stand, Mary also claimed that Matthew had forced her to watch pornography with him, and that he had bought her several 'slutty' costumes for sex, which she normally would never have worn, but for fear of her husband. If she refused, Matthew wouldn't hesitate to get physical, hitting her or even using his belt to whip her. Mary famously produced a wig and a pair of white high heels in the witness box during her cross-examination to show the court evidence of Matthew's other side.

Mary stated that she was never happy watching pornography, dressing up in sexy outfits or performing the sex acts that Matthew wanted. She went along with his ideas, however, because she didn't dare face his reaction if she didn't. 'I'd just do anything to help him stay happy.' Throughout these revelations, Mary was visibly embarrassed and uncomfortable. Clearly she would have preferred that none of them had ever come to light; but Mary felt it necessary to brave what her neighbors, and the nation, might think in order to clear her name and justify her actions.

Mary's family had been quick to corroborate her side of the story. Her father, Clark Freeman, had spoken out through Good Morning America and detailed the 'physical, mental, verbal' abuse that his daughter had suffered. Other friends came forward during the court case, and gave similar verdicts on their relationship. A friend of Mary's, Rudie Thomsen, said that '[o]ne Sunday, Mary came into the church and I looked at her and she had a black eye.' Similarly, Mary's friend Amy Redmon agreed that Matthew had been controlling: '[h]e was an authority figure, and he made the decisions basically. It was obvious.'

Conversely, Matthew's family denied that their son had been anything like Mary had depicted in her defence testimony. Matthew's father, Charles Daniel Winkler, said that his son was a kind, gentle man, who could have done nothing to justify what the defence was claiming. Diane spoke several times during the trial, lashing out at Mary: 'You've never told your girls you're sorry! Don't you think you at least owe them that?'

The dramatic story of a supposedly kindly, gentle church minister having such a sordid, cruel and abusive hidden life gripped America. The case was covered extensively on all major networks, discussed on late night panel shows

The Jury's Verdict

While the prosecutors had tried to convince the jury to convict her on a charge of first degree murder, they were unsuccessful. The jury came to their verdict by April, that year. It took them eight hours to deliberate their way to the decision; this mirrored the response of the nation, which was similarly undecided on just what punishment Mary really deserved.

Mary was found guilty of voluntary manslaughter, a charge which carries a far more lenient sentence than murder. While murderers can receive full life sentences, and in certain states receive the death penalty, the maximum sentence for voluntary manslaughter is only 6 years.

Mary showed little emotion at the verdict, but did embrace each of her relatives afterwards. In a show of support, her family had been sat in the row behind her, and all linked arms with one another to demonstrate their solidarity. Afterwards, she was taken back into custody to await sentencing.

Mary's attorney stated afterwards that Mary's testimony had been central in securing the more lenient sentence. 'I think Mary's testimony was integral in this decision. They had to hear it from Mary', Farese told the press. 'They judged her credibility and they saw that she had an abusive relationship and they made their judgment based upon that.'

For Mary, the most important implication of the verdict was that she could finally begin to think of being reunited with her children. Speaking on her behalf after the trial, Farese continued: 'We would like to do so many things to open up communication between Mary and the paternal grandparents and to get the children out of this cycle of constant upheaval over this terrible tragic event.' But the question of how long she would be in prison remained.

Mary's sentencing was scheduled for May 18th, at which point both Mary and the prosecution would have a final chance to address the court before the judge decided on the final jail term. However, the situation looked positive for Mary. Not only would the five months that she had been imprisoned awaiting trial be taken into consideration, but the judge had indicated that alternatives to incarceration would be on the table. Perhaps Mary could avoid jail time altogether.

Sentencing: The Trial at an End

Due to a scheduling error, the hearing took place around three weeks late, on June 8th.

Mary took to the stand one last time to plead for mercy. She read aloud from a prepared statement, telling Matthew's family of her sorrow and remorse for her actions. She was 'so sorry that this had happened', and would 'always miss and love' her husband. 'I ask for mercy and understanding, but I know whatever decision you reach today will be right ... I ask you to please let me go home today and be with my children.' Tabitha Freeman- Mary's sister- had also pleaded for leniency, in particular to let Mary be reunited with her children. She went as far as calling Mary 'the best example of a good person I can think of'.

Members of Matthew's family, too, took to the stand to plead their case for the prosecution. Charles and his wife were clearly hurt and in disbelief at Mary's actions both in murdering their son, and believed that Mary had purposefully smeared his name at trial. 'The monster that you have painted for the world to see? I don't think that monster existed', Diane Winkler had said.

After speaking their pieces, all that Mary, her family, and Matthew's parents could do was wait until the judge's decision. The trial- as well as the very public 'trial' that Mary had been through in the media- was finally at an end.

The defence had requested that Mary be granted full probation, or judicial diversion, both outcomes which would have meant that Mary would spent no further time in prison, and even that her record would be cleared of wrongdoing altogether. This request was denied.

After recess, Mary was told that she would spend 3 years in prison for her crime. But Circuit Judge J. Weber McCraw reduced that amount to just 210 days total in prison before she would be allowed to leave on probation. She also had that sentence reduced further, due to the fact that she had spent five months incarcerated waiting for trial.

Moreover, that time would be spent not in jail, but in a mental health centre in Tennessee. There, she would receive treatment for both her depression and post traumatic stress disorder. After such a long ordeal, with the prosecution fighting to either put Mary on death row or to imprison her indefinitely, it seemed that she had gotten off with hardly a slap on the wrist.

Steve Farese branded the sentence 'a victory': '[s]he could be in prison for life, and that's what everybody thought she was headed for to begin with.' Her other attorney, Leslie Ballin, said '[s]he'll be able to get out and fight the battle she wants to, and that is to get her children back.' Mary could finally think about the future again.

But certain signs indicated that it would not be as easy to reconcile with her children and family as she might hope. Matthew's family left the courtroom without making a comment to the press, as did the prosecution, clearly disappointed in the verdict. They gave no indication that they would be happy to open dialogue about Mary's daughters- not with the woman whom they believed to have murdered their son in cold blood.

The aftermath of Mary's release

Mary was released on August 14th, 2007. She had only been sentenced the previous June.

Upon her release, her lawyer informed the press that Mary would not be speaking with them, to maintain her privacy. During her time in the mental health facility, Mary could finally begin her attempt to win full custody of her three daughters, and she was still fighting this case at the time of her release. She had not seen her children, apart from Patricia's brief testimony as part of the case, for over a year. Throughout the case, and after Mary's release, her children were staying with Matthew's family.

Moreover, she was still fighting a $2 million dollar civil lawsuit filed by Matthew's parents. They also took legal measures, which, if successful, would have meant that the custody of Mary's children remained with them.

After her release, Mary seemed happier to her family and friends. From an outside perspective, it could be easy to claim that this was just as much due to her happiness at avoiding a jail sentence as it was to her being rid of an abuser. She was in fact living with friends at first after her release, and went back to work at a dry cleaners in McMinnville, Tenn., 200 miles from Selmer.

In the same interview as was mentioned before, Mary's sisters agreed that she had changed entirely. After years of shyness, Mary seeming unable or unwilling to show love to them for fear of her husband's violence, she seemed to finally be able to open up. 'Now it's back to the old Mary [who] loves us and doesn't care to come and hug us and gives us a kiss on the cheek.'

Since then, Mary lived in McMinnville. She has moved between jobs, working at the dry cleaners, before starting work at a nursery. She briefly dated the brother of one of her most vocal supporters, Paul Pillow; afterwards, she moved in with Wayne Cantrell, a preacher living in Smithville nearby.

Mary regained custody of her three children in 2008, but by 2010, received the news that she had multiple sclerosis. Her diagnosis came at the worst time, as she was settling down in her new life; she had not long started medical school with the desire to become a nurse, and had to quit since the work would be too demanding. She hasn't returned to work since.

One comfort for Mary was that Matthew's parents seemed close to being able to forgive her. After her diagnosis, they gave Mary some time off from parenting by taking care of the children for a weekend, which soon turned into several months. Daniel Winkler has preached several times since the events on the topic of forgiveness, although when asked by local press why he chose the topic, he has refused to answer, presumably preferring to keep those details private.

Mary, too, preferred to put the past behind her. In an interview with WAFF 48, the NBC affiliate in Huntsville AL., she stated how she would prefer to stay out of the limelight, particularly for the sake of her girls. 'Whatever reason people have any problem with me, that's fine. Everybody's entitled to their opinion, but these girls are treated for who they are, not because of what their mother's done ... They're three very fine young ladies'.

Concluding Thoughts

Some members of the public reacted with disgust at the abnormally short sentence that Mary was given, and questioned whether a husband would have been given the same leniency as Mary was. Men's rights activist Glenn Sacks publicly questioned whether a man would have been shown such leniency, and pointed to the case of Scott Peterson (who received the death penalty for the murder of his pregnant wife) to indicate that no, a man would not. He also argued that the idea of abuse had been widened to include simple criticism, and should therefore not necessarily be used as defence of murder.

Conversely, there have been many women put in prison for murdering their abusive husbands, some for much longer than Mary Winkler. The 'battered woman defense', or the preferred terminology today of 'battering and its effects', is not a genuine legal defence in itself; it can, however, be used to convince a court of diminished responsibility. Its effectiveness is due to the sympathy that it elicits from jurors, who can be convinced that abuse is a form of provocation, and the murder a form of self defense. Under this defense, Mary's short sentence makes sense.

The case has remained a touch stone with regards to spousal abuse in the U.S. A made-for-TV movie, 'The Pastor's Wife', was released in 2011. It was based on the book of the same title, written by Dianne Fanning, an award winning crime writer. The story was changed somewhat, with the inclusion of a financial subplot involving tax fraud. However, it also made use of real life interviews with people who knew the Winklers- including Matthew's parents. His mother revealed that she could never believe Mary's story. Charles admitted that Mary's story could be true, and that he could forgive her if she confessed her purposeful intention to murder Matthew.

As for the community in which the family had lived, the reaction was largely one of forgiveness. According to members of that community, the town's 'Christian roots and ... its tendency to give people the benefit of the doubt' meant that they took Mary at her word. Mary's quite life in McMinnville and Smithville similarly shows that the American public would rather leave her and her family alone after their painful ordeal.

TRACEY GRISSOM

Claiming to be a victim of rape and other abuses, a distraught Tracey Grissom would travel to her ex-husband Hunter's workplace and shoot him six times in the back, receiving a twenty-five-year life sentence for his murder.

Her defense attorney would argue that Tracey was motivated by post-traumatic stress disorder caused by her Hunter's constant abuse and sexual assaults. One jury member had even asked the judge to be lenient in her sentencing as they were not allowed to hear details of her Hunter's alleged abuses (beatings, rape, sodomy).

But what really happened in the years that led up to May 15th, 2012? Was she in fact the victim of years of abuse by a psychotic husband? Or did she want to cash in on his $100,000 life insurance policy?

INSTANT ATTRACTION

The couple would meet during a dinner party in 2003 in Tuscaloosa, Alabama. Tracey was twenty-one years old and going through a divorce. She had a son, James Michael, from the previous marriage.

Family and friends would describe the union as "love at first sight." Hunter was blown away by the young Tracey's blue eyes and facial beauty.

"For him, it was love at first sight," crime author William Phelps said. "She was gorgeous."

A whirlwind courtship would ensue and the couple would elope in 2004.

"In the beginning, it was good," Tracey told CBS' 48 hours. "We had a friendship. Just your normal, honeymoon phase marriage."

"He was fun," Tracey said. "And he was attractive."

Hunter was two years younger than Tracey, however, and his mother felt that he had jumped the gun too early in the relationship.

Her words proved to be prophetic as after only eight months into the marriage, the marriage went south.

According to Tracey, their marital problems began with Hunter's drug addiction.

"I had caught him smoking marijuana," Tracey said. "Doing illegal things could cause a problem and I couldn't risk losing my son over."

Tracey claimed that she threatened her new spouse with a divorce but Hunter gave her his word that he would stop with his drug use. She stated that the relationship improved and the decided to start a construction company together.

"I took out an equity line to start a company," Tracey said. "Which was Grissom Construction. It was all in my name."

Hunter specialized in building elaborate boat docks. He had an artistic eye and could do docks, stairs, and other accouterments. The business began to grow in short order.

"They're going to take on the world," Phelps said. "They're going to be entrepreneurs and they're gonna make it."

They then had a daughter of their own, Anna Grace. The child was a long time coming for the couple. They had been trying for a long time as Tracey had five miscarriages before Anna Grace was born.

"She was premature," Tracey recalled. "Her heart and lungs were not developed. A very stressful time."

Behind closed doors things were rocky. On the surface, however, things looked good. They had a young family and were making money.

"All-American family," Phelps said. "White-picket fence. The whole nine yards. Middle-class. Suburbia. Maybe the Prince Charming that she's been waiting for."

But again, this was only on the surface. Tracey harbored secrets of her own. One of which was her own addiction to prescription drugs.

"Psychologically, there's something going on here," Phelps said. "There's something going on behind those beautiful eyes and it ain't good."

Tracey would often turn on on the children, showing off her temper. Then she would turn on Hunter.

"This would cause friction in the marriage," Phelps said. "And where there's friction, there's fire."

SETTING THE STAGE

Tracey would later state that Hunter would "act strangely" shortly before she filed divorce. She was a registered nurse and gave him an over-the-counter drug test. According to her, Hunter tested posted for marijuana, Oxycontin, opiates, and methamphetamine.

Hunter would later be arrested for marijuana possession but his family would insist that he never did the harder drugs.

Tracey would file for divorce in the summer of 2010 after six years of marriage. According to her, this would prompt physical abuse from Hunter.

Hunter had to move out but their divorce agreement would allow him access to the home.

"In September of 2010," Tracey recalled. "That was the first time he physically hit me. It (the abuse) got progressively worse. He had made the comments that if I told anybody he would kill me. I believed him."

Hunter' co-workers and family members would have a different take on the situation, however. His co-workers remembered a time when she tracked him down at one of the jobs and made a scene.

"She's screaming, jumping on him," Hunter's co-worker said. "Said something about him having another girlfriend and used the expression about, 'You are mine. I'll kill you. I'll kill you. You are mine."

"She's borderline demonic," Hunter's mother said. " mean, I absolutely believe—that she is that troubled."

Hunter's family continued to believe that he did not abuse Tracey.

"He did not have an abusive, an angry bone in his body," Hunter's aunt Gina said. "In fact, we kind of laughed at him because he was too laid-back."

The divorce was finalized in October of 2010.

EVIDENCE OF ABUSE?

Loran Richards was the first of Tracey's friends to notice the minor injuries on her body. She would inquire about the bruises but the answers she received were always evasive. Seeing Tracey with a black eye, however, forced her to try and get more answers.

"I said, Tracey, you may have terrible luck," Richards recalled. "But nobody is so unlucky that they trip, fall down the stairs, and hit their face on a baseball in the eye socket. So don't give me a lame excuse. You don't have to give me any excuse, but let's take a picture."

Tracey broke down. She gave her friend all of the grisly details, detailing the abuse she suffered at the hands of Hunter. Loran then became her advocate, taking pictures of Tracey's injuries. She would later state that she saw blood stains and other signs of abuse at Tracey's home.

THAT FATEFUL NIGHT

Now divorced, Hunter would arrive at Tracey's home on November 22nd, 2010.

According to Tracey, he then became enraged when Tracey told him that she had spent the night with a new lover.

"He told me that he was gonna kill me," Tracey recalled. Tracey stated that she tried to escape, running into the closet in order to "get away from the kids and to pray." Tracey's eleven-year-old son from a previous relationship was in the home as was the four-year-old daughter they have together.

Hunter caught up with her and knocked her to the ground. He tied a belt around her ankles and then began choking her.

Half-conscious, Tracey alleged to have been raped and sodomized.

The brutal attack would leave Tracey unconscious. She would wake up the next morning on the bathroom floor.

"I called Hunter," Tracey recalled. "I told him that I was bleeding and that I was hurt and that I needed help. And he told me, 'Fuck you. I hope you die.'"

Tracey wound up in the emergency room after the attack. Hospital records would show that she had a laceration on her head, bruises, and ligature marks on her feet.

Tracey would then be referred to the Turning Point domestic violence center.

Marian Waters would describe Tracey's injuries as among the worst she had ever seen in a twenty-year career.

Waters would testify that Tracey had suffered a horrific assault. She described her mental state as typical of someone who had just been raped; fearful, jumpy, fearing for her life.

Tracey had suffered a hematoma on her side that was the side of a grapefruit. She also claimed to have experienced rectal nerve damage which would require surgery as well as torn vaginal muscles requiring her to have a hysterectomy.

Police were called and Hunter would be arrested for rape, sodomy, kidnapping and domestic violence.

"And at that point, I feared for my life," Tracey recalled. "And I feared for my children's life."

A HIDDEN AGENDA

Hunter would be freed on bail but Tracey got a restraining order against him. She bought a gun and did not go anywhere unarmed.

She took photos of her injuries on the night of the alleged attack and texted them to Loran. Later, they would take more pictures.

Angered, Hunter would stop paying her spousal and child support. Tracey, however, may have had another scenario in mind for obtaining money.

She had forced Hunter to take out a $103,000 life insurance policy around the time their daughter was born.

On May 24, 2012, the day before Tracey shot Hunter, she would place a call to MetLife that was recorded.

"Thank you for calling MetLife, this is Pam. May I please have your name?"

"Tracey Grissom."

Tracey would then explain that she was angry that her husband stopped making payments on his policy. During their divorce proceedings, he had agreed to continue paying the premiums. Tracey stated she was calling to make sure that they had the correct address on file.

"Is there anything else I can do for you today?

"That's gonna be it!" Tracey said, hanging up.

"Well, May 14th was just like any other day," Tracey said, explaining the call to the insurance company. "However, I had moved four different times. Me and my children were running. We were running from Hunter. So I had called the company to let them know that they had my old address and to make an address change."

FALSE RAPE?

Shelly Standridge was hired by Hunter to defend him in the rape case. She would state that Hunter denied raping or even assaulting Tracey that night. Hunter did, however, admit to the fact that he and his wife had consensual sex that night...Rough consensual sex.

"So that night," Standridge said. "Hunter said that she was depressed and claiming she was going to kill herself. She was saying she wanted their relationship to work."

So she undressed in front of him. Her beauty was always impossible for Hunter to resist.

The two had sex despite Hunter having a new girlfriend at home.

Hunter's aunt, Gina, believed that Tracey wanted to kill Hunter before the rape case went to court.

"He had a new girlfriend, he was living with her," Phelps said. "He was moving on with his life. Hunter would claim that Tracey was jealous, obsessive, even stalked them."

"Hunter had moved on," Hunter's aunt said. "There was some court dates coming up that would prove that Hunter was innocent. There were court dates coming up that he would get visitation to his daughter. She had a lot to lose."

Tracey was on the anti-anxiety drug Klonopin. Hunter would tell his attorney that Tracey would take more than her prescribed dose. Because of this, she fell and cut her head. Hunter would then leave the house around 10:30 pm and go to his father's house. Tracey would call him hours later, at 3:20 am.

Hunter would state that Tracey had called to threaten him. She told him if he didn't want the responsibility of the children then she would make it where he would never be able to see them again.

Hunter's attorney did not know what Tracey's motive was for crying rape. She was very upset that he had a girlfriend.

MORE LIES...

Hunter would be arrested nearly twelve hours later, to his total shock.

Tracey would give her side of the story to the police which later is proven to be false.

She would tell police that Hunter had thrown her against the bathtub around 10 pm and claim to be unconscious until 4 am the next morning.

"But her phone records show she was on the phone all night, so she was never unconscious," Standridge said. "She was also using her data at 10:42 that night. She was using it again at 10:50 that night. ... She sends a text to her boyfriend at 1:49 am. She sends a text to her friend at 2:07 am. She sends another text to her boyfriend at 2:07 am."

Tracey would blame the calls on Hunter.

"All I do know is I was not the only person using my phone that night," Tracey said, suggesting that Hunter used her phone.

Medical records would show that Tracey's head wound was "purely superficial".

Only one suture was needed.

Furthermore, there was nothing on the medical record to support the fact that Tracey experienced vaginal and rectal tears. She did have bruises on her ankle and legs but the photos taken by police at the emergency room would not resemble the same photos that Tracey and her friend Loran would take days later. In the photos taken at the emergency room, an area of Tracey's body has no bruises. Days later, there is discoloration.

Tracey's attorney would blame the discrepancy on "blood thinners" which would cause Tracey to bruise easily.

There was also a discrepancy in her phone records. She would take a photo of her inner thigh, a deep bruise. This area of her body was not photographed by police during her emergency room visit. But on December 9th, almost two weeks later, Tracey took a photo of her inner thigh with the deep bruise

"He (Hunter) told me that he would make it to where nobody would ever want me," Tracey said after a 2010 attack. "I didn't report it because I thought he would kill me."

THE FINAL STRAW

Tracey woke up pissed on May 15th, 2012.

Hunter had been ordered to pay $2,100 a month for the rest of his life. He was not complying with the court order claiming that he was "out of work."

Tracey stated that she was on her way to a job interview when she saw a Grissom Construction sign out of the corner of her eye.

She stated that her initial plan was to take a photograph of Hunter at the job site in order to show proof that he was working as part of her litigation.

"I was getting ready to take the picture and when I looked up he was standing almost directly towards the front of the boat trailer," Tracey said. "He was looking back directly at me. He had this face, that's like mean - just, I don't know how to describe it. I mean, I see it over and over like it's right there all the time. He flipped me the bird, which to me was kinda like, 'Yeah I'm workin. Screw you.' And at that point, I panicked. At that point, I didn't know what else to do except to defend myself."

Tracey started firing. The first shot hit Hunter in the arm. He started to run and she fired again repeatedly. One of the bullets punctured Hunter's heart and he died of massive internal bleeding.

William Dockery was working with Hunter and was an eyewitness to the shooting. Hunter had turned to Dockery before the shooting and told him to "call the law". Before Dockery could pick up his cell phone, Tracey had commenced shooting.

Tracey then pulled out her own cell phone and called the cops on herself. She tearfully described that she had just murdered her husband.

CONFESSION

Tracey told detectives exactly what was going through her mind when she came upon Hunter at the construction site.

"Tell me about what happened," the detective said. "What led up to...what's going on."

"In November of 2010, he beat me unconscious and raped me...and, and left me for dead....and, and I finally pressed charges against him and he told me that he would make my life a living hell...and that's what he's done."

"What, what happened this morning that led up to you going..."

"I was going to work and I saw him...and he's been claiming that he-he's not working. And, so I pulled in there to take a picture of him...cause it was the truck that's still in my name...and the boat that's still in my name...and the trailer that's still in my name...He just stared at me and flipped me off...and I just went in there and shot him...I just shot him, I shot him, and I shot him."

Tracey would be distraught and tearful during her interrogation room confession. A few weeks later, however, she would call the insurance company to let them know that Hunter had died.

"Well, I was actually calling because I didn't know what I needed to do ... Hunter passed away May 15th and I actually am going a court case right now because it was due to self-defense..."

Hunter's family went ballistic over this. Tracey would claim that she had no money but she continued to pay his life insurance premiums.

"Even through the times when she's screamin' that she's destitute and has no money ... she continued to pay life insurance premium," Hunter's mother said.

"I don't think my sister concocted a story," Tracey's sister said. "Just so she could get insurance money. ... But that's all they (the prosecution) had."

THE TRIAL

Tracey's allegations of rape and sodomy would not be allowed in court testimony. She was allowed, however, to detail the effects of Hunter's abuse on her were.

Taking the stand, Tracey would lift up her shirt in court and show herself wearing a colostomy bag. She stated that she had undergone several surgeries after her husband's daily rapes wherein she suffered permanent rectal and vaginal damage.

Hunter's family was then allowed to speak at the hearing.

"This tremendous loss has changed me," Hunter's mother, Melanie Garner said. "And I don't know how to change back."

Chloe, Hunter's sister, had a victim's services officer read her letter in court.

"Tracey is psychotic," Chloe wrote. "She is the most selfish person human being on this earth."

"Every mother should pray every night that your son doesn't fall in love with someone like Tracey," Hunter's aunt, Gina Grissom said. "There have been lots of allegations against Hunter. We've never believed anything that has come out of her (Tracey's) mouth."

His aunt then looked directly at Tracey.

"Hunter was proud of his name. Why would you still choose to use our name, and bring it down?" suggesting that if Tracey hated him so much why didn't she go revert to her maiden name after the divorce.

The jurors would find Tracey guilty of murder. She would be sentenced to twenty-five years in prison.

One of the jurors, Janice Kelly, would contact Grissom's attorney Warren Freeman the morning after the trial. She had remorse over her decision and said that she wouldn't have convicted her had they had the rapes and abuse allegations been introduced as evidence.

"I feel I made a mistake," Kelly said. "If I had to do it over again, we'd have had a hung jury. We didn't get her side. She did not get a fair trial."

"We voted to convict because there was no dispute that Tracey shot Hunter," the jury foreman wrote in a letter that was addressed in the courthouse. "Jurors didn't believe prosecutor claims that she did it in order to collect a life insurance policy. We felt the shooting was a crime of passion, not for financial gain and that she should be sentenced accordingly. I wish we had seen evidence of the rape allegation. We feel that she just 'lost it.'"

"It's not fair, it's not fair!" Tracey sobbed as she was led out of the courthouse and to jail.

"We think the sentencing was too harsh," Tracey's attorney Warren Freeman said. "Considering you have the foreperson of the jury actually saying, we don't feel like she should be punished according to being found guilty of murder. Let's just say that there will be a basis for a new trial, and part of it will be something that the jurors saw that they weren't supposed to see and I'm going to just leave it at that until I file my motion."

"My son died running for his life," Hunter's mother said. "I don't know what was running through his mind but I hear him say 'momma.'"

"People who think that I murdered him in cold blood," Tracey said. "Either don't know the whole story or don't know everything that's happened.

Tracey was asked on CBS' 48 hours if she regretted pulling the trigger on that fateful day.

"No," she said flatly. "Because if I hadn't I would be dead. I truly believe that."

"She has a way of making everything she does look right," Hunter's aunt, Gina scoffed.

TED BUNDY

Ted Bundy is one of the most prolific serial killers of the 20th century, having kidnapped, raped, and murdered at least 36 attractive young women between 1973 and 1978 in Colorado, Oregon, Utah, Florida, and Washington; however, many assert that this figure could be much higher. He had also kept some of his victims' body parts—including heads—as trophies in a utility shed behind his Utah home, as well having engaged in necrophilia with decomposing corpses which he would groom and apply makeup.

A master manipulator and classic antisocial personality, Bundy escaped custody twice; once from court during his first murder trial and the second time from the Garfield County Jail in Colorado by sawing a hole in his cell ceiling. He was placed on the FBI's Ten Most Wanted list and was later arrested in Florida in February 1978 after stealing a car. He was sentenced to death in 1979 for the murder of two Florida State University sorority sisters, and again in 1980 for another murder.

Very charismatic and handsome, Bundy exploited these characteristics heavily with his young female victims in an effort to earn their sympathy trust. He would often approach potential victims in public places, feigning injury or impersonating an authority figure before overpowering them—usually by hitting them in the head with a crowbar—taking them to secluded locations, and raping and murdering them. Sometimes he would simply break into young women's homes and bludgeon them while they slept.

Bundy was originally incarcerated for aggravated kidnapping and attempted assault in 1975 in Utah; however, his list of homicide victims continued to grow. He escaped from custody twice in Colorado and subsequently committed three more murders before finally being apprehended in Florida in 1978. Ted Bundy was sentenced to death and was executed in the electric chair at Raiford Prison in Starke, Florida, on 24 January 1989.

Early Life

Theodore Robert Bundy—originally Theodore Robert Cowell—was born on 24 November 1946 at the Elizabeth Lund Home for Unwed Mothers in Burlington, Vermont. The social stigma of being a single mother was great at that time so Bundy's mother, Louise Cowell, took her infant son to live with her parents—Samuel and Eleanor—in Philadelphia where young Ted took on the Cowell surname and was told that they were, in fact, his parents and that his mother was his sister. Eventually, Bundy discovered the truth and harbored lifelong resentment toward his mother for lying to him.

Bundy's paternity has never been definitively proven. His birth certificate lists his father as Lloyd Marshall, an Air Force veteran and salesman; however, Louise has claimed that she was "seduced by 'a sailor'" whose name "may have been Jack Worthington" but nobody by that name was ever found in Navy or merchant marines records. Compounding the problem is that Bundy's grandfather, Samuel Cowell, has been rumored to be his biological father; thus making Bundy the product of incest; however, again, there is no evidence of this.

In interviews, Bundy spoke highly of his grandparents, especially expressing a fondness for his grandfather even though other family members described Samuel as a tyrannical bully and bigot who beat his wife and dog, abused his daughters, harmed neighborhood cats, and would sometimes "speak aloud to unseen presences". Bundy's grandmother was timid and obedient and was treated for her depression with electroconvulsive therapy.

Bundy exhibited disturbing behavior from a young age. At the age of three, he was alleged to have surrounded his sleeping aunt, Julia, with household knives—blades pointed toward her—and smiled at her when she had awakened.

In 1950, when Bundy was only four, Louise changed both her and her son's surname to Nelson and moved them both to Tacoma, Washington, to live with cousins Jane and Alan Scott. In 1951, Louise met hospital cook Johnny Culpepper Bundy at a church singles night and they married later that year. Johnny formally adopted young Ted and he adopted the last name of Bundy. Even with efforts to include young Ted in family activities along with his four half-siblings—who he was often left to babysit—he always was distant. Later, Bundy would tell his girlfriend that Johnny wasn't his real dad, wasn't smart enough, and didn't make much money.

Bundy confessed that he "chose to be alone" as an adolescent and neither had any natural inclination to develop any close friendships nor knew what drove people to be friends in the first place. He would later say that he "hit a wall" and his inability to comprehend social behavior stunted his social development, rendering him required to adopt a façade of social activity. He was terribly shy, self-doubting, and uncomfortable in social situations and often teased for being different. Despite this, he was a good student at Woodrow Wilson High School, was active in a local Methodist church, and was even involved with a local Boy Scout troop.

Bundy would also admit—while on death row—that a part of him as a young child was "fascinated by images of sex and violence" and he called this part "the entity". He enjoyed reading crime books and detective magazines, particularly those that contained descriptions of sexual violence and pictures of dead bodies. Later, before his execution, he would admit that pornography was central in shaping who he was.

Throughout high school Bundy loved to ski and was very good at it; however, his pursuit of this hobby was usually accomplished with stolen equipment and forged lift tickets. He was also arrested on at least two occasions on suspicion of auto theft and burglary but when he turned 18 his juvenile record was expunged. Stealing, for Bundy, did not involve any guilt and, in fact, he had a sense of entitlement about the entire thing. He often said that the thrill of taking possession of something he wanted without remorse was exciting. Many speculate that his "taking" of his victims represented this same concept and provided him with the same rush. Compounding the problem was his sense of entitlement and cunning ability to lie about everything which demonstrates a common trait among psychopaths.

Bundy graduated high school in 1965 and was awarded a scholarship by the University of Puget Sound where he started that fall, taking courses in Oriental studies and psychology. After two semesters he transferred to the University of Washington in Seattle.

He obtained employment as a stock boy and bagger at a Safeway store on Queen Anne Hill, in addition to other odd jobs. As part of his psychology curricula, he would work as a night-shift volunteer at Seattle's Suicide Hot Line where he met and worked Ann Rule who would later become among the world's foremost true crime writers and who penned a biography about Bundy—that was also partly autobiographical about her working relationship with him—entitled *The Stranger Beside Me* (1980).

While in college, circa 1968, Bundy began a relationship with fellow student "Stephanie Brooks" (a pseudonym); however, after she graduated in 1968 and prepared to move back home to California she broke up with Bundy due to what she described as his lack of ambition and immaturity. Bundy was heartbroken after this and, interestingly, all of his victims bore some resemblance to Brooks; particularly the fact that Brooks and all of his victims had long dark hair which they wore parted down the middle.

Shortly thereafter, Bundy returned to Burlington—his birthplace—and learned the truth of his parentage. This discovery made him more dominant and focused.

He managed the Seattle office of Nelson Rockefeller's presidential campaign in 1968 and attended the 1968 Republican convention in Miami, Florida. He reenrolled at the University of Washington with a major in psychology. He became popular among his professors as he was an honor student and also began a relationship with Elizabeth Kloepfer in 1969. Kloepfer was a divorced secretary with a young daughter and the two dated for the next six years until he went to prison in 1976.

Bundy graduated in 1972 with a degree in psychology and went to work for the state Republican Party.

In the fall of 1973, Bundy enrolled in the University of Utah Law School but did poorly because of poor attendance and, consequently, dropped out the following spring.

While in California on a business trip in the summer of 1973, Bundy found his ex-girlfriend "Stephanie Brooks" and the change in his look and attitude was appealing to her. Bundy courted Brooks the rest of the year—while still involved with Kloepfer—and proposed to her, only to dump Brooks shortly after the new year, likely in retaliation for her breaking his heart years earlier. The breakup wreaked havoc on Bundy who became obsessed with her and this obsession "would span his lifetime and lead to a series of events that would shock the world".

Mere weeks later, Bundy began his first murderous rampage in Washington; however, many Bundy experts assert that he likely starting killing in his teens. One case involved eight-year-old Ann Marie Burr from Tacoma who disappeared from her home in 1961 when Bundy was 14. Burr's house was on Bundy's newspaper delivery route and her father was positive that he saw Bundy near a construction site ditch on the nearby University of Puget Sound campus the day his daughter vanished. Despite other potentially incriminating circumstantial evidence, Bundy remains merely a suspect due to a lack of consensus by law enforcement personnel as to whether they believe he actually did it or not. Bundy has always denied killing her.

Shortly before his execution, Bundy did, in fact, tell his attorney that his first attempt at kidnapping was in 1969 and his first "actual murder" occurred "sometime in 1972". While he was a suspect in the December 1973 murder of Kathy Devine in Washington, DNA analysis exonerated him and her true murderer was convicted in 2002.

Bundy's earliest identified murders were committed in 1974 when he was 27.

Bundy was a handsome and charismatic guy, particularly to his young female victims and he exploited these characteristics fully. He was also an adept chameleon, able to blend in and feign belonging which increased his threat to the attractive brunette women he targeted as his victims. This charm and his adroitness at lying and manipulation made him extremely dangerous.

Known Murder Victims

Karen Sparks (often referred to as Joni Lenz), 18 (survived)

On 4 January 1974, 18-year-old Karen Sparks/Joni Lenz was found by her roommates when she didn't emerge from her bedroom that morning. They were not prepared for what horrific sights they saw. Sparks had been beaten badly and a bed rod ripped from the bed was "savagely rammed into her vagina". Sparks was transported to the hospital in a coma and suffered damages which continue to plague her.

However, she was one of the lucky few victims to survive an attack by Bundy.

Lynda Ann Healy, 21

A very accomplished and beautiful young woman, 21-year-old Lynda Healy announced ski conditions for all of the western Washington resorts on the radio. A senior at the University of Washington, she came from a good family, loved to sing, and was majoring in psychology. She shared a house with four other young women near the university. On 31 January, Healy and some friends went to a tavern and then home to bed. Her roommate in the next room never heard any sounds emanating from Healy's room that night.

The following morning when she didn't emerge from her bedroom after her alarm clock sounded at its usual 5:30 a.m. to go to work—and her job called looking for her—her roommate noticed that her bed was made in a peculiar way. Further inspection showed that the top sheet and a pillowcase were missing, a small bloodstain that was the same type as Lynda's was on the pillow and the bottom sheet, and a bloody nightgown was hanging in her closet. One of her outfits was missing. Also worrisome was that one of the doors was unlocked.

Initially, due to the absence of fingerprint, hair, or fiber evidence, police did not suspect foul play; however, later, they did come to realize that an intruder came in, removed Healy's nightgown and dressed her in another outfit, made the bed, wrapped her up, and took her out of the house.

Donna Gail Manson, 19

On 12 March, in Olympia, 19-year-old Evergreen State College student Donna Manson was kidnapped and murdered.

Susan Elaine Rancourt, 18

On 17 April, Susan Rancourt, 18, disappeared from the Central Washington State College campus in Ellensburg while walking across campus, alone, at night.

Later, two other female coeds would report meeting a good-looking man with his arm in a cast—one the night Rancourt disappeared and one three nights earlier—who asked for assistance with carrying books to his VW Beetle.

Roberta Kathleen "Kathy" Parks, 22

Kathy Parks, 22, was last seen on 6 May on the Oregon State University campus in Corvallis en route to meeting friends for coffee.

Brenda Carol Ball, 22

22-year-old Brenda Ball was last seen leaving the Flame Tavern in Burien, Oregon on 1 June.

Georgeann Hawkins, 18

In the early morning hours of 11 June, University of Washington student and a member of Kappa Alpha Theta Georgeann Hawkins, 18, left her boyfriend's dormitory en route to her sorority house through an alley. She was never seen again; however, witnesses later stated they had seen a man with a leg cast struggling to carry a briefcase in that area. Another female coed reported that he had asked her for help in carrying his briefcase to his VW Beetle.

Bundy later confessed to having lured Hawkins to his car, clubbed her with a tire iron he had hidden underneath his vehicle, and then took her elsewhere to rape and strangle her to death.

Janice Ann Ott, 23, and Denise Marie Naslund, 19

On 14 July, Janet Ott, 23, and Denise Naslund, 19, were abducted mere hours apart from Lake Sammamish State Park in Issaquah, Washington, in broad daylight. On that day, eight different witnesses reported seeing a handsome young man with his arm in a sling who called himself "Ted" and who asked several women for help unloading a sailboat from his VW Beetle. One witness said she walked with him for a ways but didn't see a sailboat and then declined to help him. Other witnesses stated that they saw the man approach Ott and she was observed walking away with him.

Naslund disappeared four hours later.

At this point, police in King County put up fliers with the suspected murderer's description all over the Seattle area. One of Bundy's psychology professors, former coworker Ann Rule, and Bundy's girlfriend Elizabeth Kloepfer reported him as a possible suspect. In fact, Kloepfer (who since changed her surname to Kendall and penned a book called *The Phantom Prince: My Life with Ted Bundy* in 1981) told the Seattle Police Department that her boyfriend "might be involved" in the recent Seattle murders. She called again later that autumn with more information and agreed to give them recent pictures of Bundy to be shown to witnesses; however, many of them could not positively identify him.

Ott's and Naslund's remains were found on 7 September off Interstate 90 near Issaquah, only one mile from the park where they were abducted. Near the women's remains was an extra femur and vertebrae which Bundy confessed before his execution belonged to Hawkins.

Between 1 March and 3 March 1975, the skulls and jawbones belonging to Healy, Rancourt, Parks, and Ball were found just east of Issaquah on Taylor Mountain. Bundy confessed in his death row interview that he kept the decapitated heads of these four victims in his apartment for some time and that he would revisit this dump site often to engage in sex with the corpses until decomposition became too great to continue. Bundy also admitted that he dumped Manson's body there as well—but burned her skull in his girlfriend's fireplace—however, no trace of her was ever recovered.

Other trophies discovered when Bundy's apartment was searched include photographs of his victims and a large bag of women's clothing.

Nancy Wilcox, 16

Bundy began the University of Utah Law School in the autumn of 1974. On 2 October 1974, 16-year-old Nancy Wilcox disappeared from Holladay, Utah. She was last seen in a VW Beetle.

Melissa Smith, 17

On 18 October, 17-year-old Melissa Smith—the daughter of Midvale, Utah's Police Chief Louis Smith—disappeared after leaving a pizza parlor. Nine days later she was found strangled, raped, and sodomized.

Laura Aime, 17

17-year-old Laura Aime disappeared from a Halloween party in Lehi, Utah. Her naked corpse was found on Thanksgiving Day by hikers near a river in the Wasatch Mountains. She had been beaten about the head and face with a crowbar and was raped and sodomized. The lack of blood at the crime scene indicated that she was likely killed elsewhere and dumped in this location. Police found no other physical evidence.

Carol DaRonch, 18 (survived)

On 8 November, 18-year-old Carol DaRonch was shopping at the Fashion Place Mall in Salt Lake City, Utah, and was approached by a man in the Sears parking lot who claimed to be a police officer named Officer Roseland. He told her that her car had been stolen and that he would take her to the police station to retrieve it. He took her to his VW Beetle and she became suspicious and asked him for identification. He quickly flashed a gold badge and she got in but refused his order to fasten her seat belt. After a short distance, Bundy pulled over and attempted to place handcuffs on DaRonch but only managed one wrist. He also attempted to hit her with a crowbar which she was able to catch before it hit her head. DaRonch fought back, kicking him in the groin, and as the car was speeding away she jumped out of it.

DaRonch flagged down another car and they took her to the police who confirmed there was no Officer Roseland. Police were able to obtain a description of the assailant and his car and a blood sample from DaRonch's coat. Type O; the same as Bundy's.

Debra Kent, 17

Mere hours after losing DaRonch Bundy abducted 17-year-old Debra "Debi" Kent from the parking lot of a school in Bountiful, Utah, as she was leaving a school play. She had told her parents she was going to pick up her brother at the bowling alley and she would be back to pick them up soon but never returned. She didn't even make it to her car which was still in the parking lot. Police found a small handcuff key in the parking lot and when they tried the key in the handcuffs DaRonch was wearing, it was a perfect fit.

A month later a man called the police and told them that he saw a tan VW Beetle speeding away from the high school parking lot the night Kent disappeared.

Shortly before he was to be executed, Bundy confessed that he dumped Kent's body near Fairview, Utah. After an intense search of the area, a human kneecap which was consistent with someone of Kent's age and size was found; however, DNA analysis was not conducted.

Caryn Campbell, 23

Bundy's first murder of 1975 occurred on 12 January. 23-year-old Michigan nurse Caryn Campbell disappeared between her hotel's lounge and her room while on a ski trip with her fiancé, Dr. Raymond Gadowski, and his two children, in Snowmass, Colorado. Frantic Gadowski called the police the next morning but a search proved futile.

Nearly a month later—and only a few short miles from where she went missing—a recreational worker discovered Campbell's nude body near the road. Animal damage to her body made it difficult to determine the exact cause of death; however, there was evidence of repeated, crushing blows to her head by a sharp instrument. Some of the blows were so violent that one of her teeth separated from the gums.

Julie Cunningham, 26

On 15 March, 26-year-old Vail ski instructor Julie Cunningham disappeared on her way to a nearby tavern. Bundy confessed in prison that he used his crutches ploy to approach Cunningham to ask for her help carrying ski boots to his car before he clubbed her with his crowbar, handcuffed her, and took her to a secluded location where strangled her.

Denise Oliverson, 25

25-year-old Denise Oliverson vanished in Grand Junction on 6 April while riding her bicycle to visit her parents.

Lynette Culver, 13

13-year-old Lynette Culver was abducted from her school playground at Alameda Junior High School in Pocatello, Idaho.

Susan Curtis, 15

Once Bundy returned to Utah, 15-year-old Susan Curtis vanished on 28 June while walking alone to the Brigham Young University dormitories during a youth conference she was attending. Bundy confessed to her murder minutes before his execution.

The bodies of Cunningham, Oliverson, Culver, and Curtis have never been found.

First Arrest, Trial, and Escapes

Bundy was first arrested on 16 August 1975 in Salt Lake City for failure to stop his vehicle for police. A search of his car unearthed a crowbar, handcuffs, ski mask, trash bags, an icepick, and other items the officer thought were burglary tools. The always calm and collected Bundy explained reasons why he had the items such as that he used the mask for skiing and had found the handcuffs in a dumpster; however, Detective Jerry Thompson connected Bundy and his Volkswagen to the DaRonch kidnapping and other missing girls and searched his apartment.

The search yielded a brochure of Colorado ski resorts with a checkmark by where Campbell had disappeared. Bundy was brought in for a lineup before DaRonch and other witnesses at the time DaRonch was kidnapped and they all identified him as Officer Roseland, as well as the man lurking about on the night Debbie Kent vanished.

After a week-long trial, Bundy was convicted on 1 March 1976 of kidnapping DaRonch and was sentenced to 15 years in Utah State Prison. Bundy was then extradited to Colorado to stand trial for murder.

He was able to escape custody twice before his eventual final arrest in Florida. The first escape occurred on 7 June 1977, when he was transported from the Garfield County Jail in Glenwood Springs, Colorado, to Pitkin County Courthouse in Aspen for his preliminary hearing. As he was serving as his own attorney, the judge excused him from being handcuffed and shackled. During a recess Bundy asked if he could research his case in the courthouse's law library. Hiding behind a bookcase he jumped from a second-story window, spraining his ankle when he landed. After shedding his suit, he simply walked through the town of Aspen as roadblocks were being erected before hiking southward on Aspen Mountain.

Near its summit he burglarized a cabin and stole clothing, food, and a rifle before heading toward Crested Butte; however, Bundy became lost and ended up wandering aimlessly for two days before breaking into a camping trailer on Maroon Lake where he took more food and a parka. Bundy then walked back toward Aspen and stole a car parked at the Aspen Golf Course. Two police officers noticed him weaving in traffic and pulled over the six-day fugitive. In the car were maps of the mountains around Aspen that the prosecutor was using to demonstrate where victim Caryn Campbell's body was found. As Bundy was his own attorney, he had the right of discovery to this evidence, thus demonstrating that he had planned his escape.

Bundy's second escape occurred on 30 December 1977, after having his motion for a change of venue to Denver accepted but with the venue being Colorado Springs instead; a city that had historically been hostile to murder suspects. He had managed to acquire the jail's floor plan and a hacksaw blade from other inmates, as well as $500 in cash smuggled in over a six-month period by visitors—particularly one Carole Ann Boone. In the evening while other inmates were showering, Bundy sawed a one-foot-square hole in his cell's ceiling—behind the steel bars—and was able to fit through it into the crawlspace above after losing 35 pounds. Prior to his actual escape, Bundy "practiced" and multiple reports of possible movement in the ceiling's crawlspace were, curiously, never investigated.

On the night of his escape, Bundy piled files and books under his covers in his bunk to look like his sleeping body, climbed into the crawlspace, broke through the jail's ceiling which, incidentally, was the chief jailer's apartment who just happened to be out for the evening with his wife. Bundy stole some street clothes and casually sauntered out the front door.

Bundy stole a car and drove east; however, the car broke down on Colorado's Interstate 70. A passing motorist gave him a ride into Vail where he caught a bus to Denver and then took a flight to Chicago, Illinois. From there he took an Amtrak train to Ann Arbor, Michigan.

His escape was discovered over 17 hours after the fact at noon on New Year's Eve.

Lisa Levy, 20, Margaret Bowman, 21, Karen Chandler (survived), Kathy Kleiner Deshields (survived)

On 15 January 1978—after Bundy had escaped from jail in Colorado, he traveled to Tallahassee, Florida, and attacked Chi Omega sorority sisters at Florida State University. At approximately 3:00 a.m. he entered the sorority house where he raped and strangled 20-year-old Lisa Levy to death; bludgeoned 21-year-old Margaret Bowman to death; and also bludgeoned Karen Chandler and Kathy Kleiner—both of whom survived.

The entire rampage took only 30 minutes.

Cheryl Thomas (survived)

That same morning, a mere eight blocks from the Chi Omega sorority house, Bundy attacked Cheryl Thomas in her bed and bludgeoned her with a wooden club, severely injuring her.

Kimberly Leach, 12

On 9 February, Bundy kidnapped 12-year-old Kimberly Leach from her junior high school in Lake City, Florida. Her raped, murdered, and dumped body was found in Suwannee River State Park underneath a small pig shed.

Bundy then stole another VW Beetle and left Tallahassee, traveling west across the Florida panhandle.

Florida Arrest

On 15 February 1978 shortly after 1:00 a.m., Bundy was stopped by Pensacola police officer David Lee who learned that the vehicle was stolen. After a brief scuffle, Lee had subdued and restrained Bundy and then took him to jail. During the transport, Bundy allegedly told Lee that he wished the officer would have killed him. Once his identity was confirmed, Bundy was transported to Tallahassee and charged with the Tallahassee and Lake City murders.

Florida Trials and Convictions

Among the most damning evidence during Bundy's June 1979 Chi Omega murder trial were bite marks found on Lisa Levy's left buttock which matched a plaster cast taken from Bundy's mouth. Additionally, Chi Omega sister Nita Neary was returning home late that night and saw Bundy as he left. She was able to identify him in court.

Bundy was convicted on all counts and sentenced to death.

In 1980, Bundy stood trial for the Kimberly Leach murder. Again, he was convicted, this time based upon fiber evidence and an eyewitness who saw him leading Leach away from the school. Bundy was, again, sentenced to death.

After his sentences he sought a stay of execution or commutation of his death sentences to life imprisonment by having one of his legal advocates contact his victims' families to ask them to ask for mercy in order to find out where their loved ones' remains were. This ploy for more time failed.

Execution

Bundy ultimately met his demise in Raiford Prison's electric chair on 24 January 1989.

Shortly before his widely-publicized execution, Bundy confessed to 36 murders in seven states; however, many believe that the total number is much higher. Also before his execution, Bundy contacted Dr. James Dobson, psychologist and founder of the Christian evangelical organization Focus on the Family, and agreed to a television interview the day before his execution. In it, Bundy described the influence of pornography on his behavior. While not expressly blaming pornography for his behavior, Bundy did say that pornographic materials shaped and molded his behavior and he would gradually need more violent, graphic, and explicit material to achieve the same "high"; not unlike a drug addict. He claimed that while murdering he was "possessed by 'something ... awful and alien'" and the brutal urge was indescribable. He also claimed that alcohol helped remove the initial boundary for him to commit his first murder. Bundy also admitted that although he believed he deserved the death penalty, he didn't want to die.

Even today, Bundy remains a suspect in a number of open homicide cases and is likely responsible for other victims who will never be identified. In 1987 he confided to Keppel that there were some murders that he would "never talk about" because they were committed too close to home, involved victims who were very young, or were too close to family. Said victims include the aforementioned Ann Marie Burr who Bundy repeatedly denied having murdered; however, Keppel noticed that Burr fits all three of Bundy's "no discussion" categories. In 2011, forensic testing of material from the Burr crime scene did not have enough intact DNA sequences to compare to Bundy's.

Additional potential victims include flight attendants Lisa E. Wick and Lonnie Trumbull, both 20, who were bludgeoned with a piece of wood while asleep in their Seattle home on 23 June 1966 that was very near the Safeway store where Bundy worked at the time, and where the victims regularly shopped. Trumbull did not make it and Wick suffered permanent memory loss.

On 30 May 1969 college friends Susan Davis and Elizabeth Perry, both 19, who were on vacation in Atlantic City, New Jersey—just 60 miles south of Philadelphia—were found stabbed to death in the woods three days later.

On 19 July 1971, 24-year-old elementary school teacher and motel maid Rita Curran was murdered in her basement apartment in Burlington, Vermont. She had been bludgeoned, raped, and strangled. The motel where she worked part-time was adjacent to the Elizabeth Lund Home where Bundy was born and certain similarities to his other crime scenes made Bundy a suspect.

21-year-old Joyce LePage was last seen alive on 22 July 1971 on the Washington State University campus. Nine months later her skeleton was found wrapped in military blankets, carpeting, and rope, at the bottom of a Pullman, Washington, ravine.

On 29 June 1973, 17-year-old Rita Lorraine Jolly disappeared from West Linn, Oregon while 24-year-old Vicki Lynn Hollar disappeared from Eugene, Oregon, on 20 August of that same year. Bundy had confessed to two Oregon homicides but did not identify the victims.

Brenda Joy Baker, 14, was last seen hitchhiking near Puyallup, Washington on 27 May 1974 and her body would be discovered a month later in Millersylvania State Park.

19-year-old Wisconsin native Sandra Jean Weaver who had been living in Tooele, Utah, was last seen on 1 July 1974 in Salt Lake City. Her nude body was found the following day in Grand Junction, Colorado.

20-year-old Carol Valenzuela was last seen hitchhiking near Vancouver, Washington, on 2 August 1974 and her remains were found two months later in a shallow grave south of Olympia; along with the remains of another female who was later identified as 17-year-old Martha Morrison who was last seen in Eugene, Oregon, on 1 September 1974. During this time, Bundy drove from Seattle to Salt Lake City and could have conceivably passed through both towns; however, there is no definitive evidence.

Bundy is also a suspect in Melanie Suzanne Cooley's disappearance on 15 April 1975 after leaving Nederland High School in Nederland, Colorado. Her beaten and strangled corpse was discovered on 2 May by road maintenance workers nearby in Coal Creek Canyon. Whereas gas receipts place Bundy in Golden that day—not far from Nederland—the Jefferson County Sheriff's Office has classified her murder as a cold case.

On 1 July 1975, Shelly Kay Robertson, 24, failed to show up for work in Golden, Colorado, and her nude, decomposed corpse was found in August inside of a mine on Berthoud Pass near Winter Park. While gas station receipts place Bundy in the area, there is no direct evidence as to his complicity.

23-year-old Nancy Perry Baird disappeared from the Farmington, Utah, service station where she worked on 4 July 1975. She officially remains a missing person and Bundy has repeatedly denied involvement.

Finally, 17-year-old Debbie Smith was last seen in February 1976 in Salt Lake City before the DaRonch trial. Her body was found near the airport on 1 April 1976.

Aftermath

During the Kimberly Leach trial, Bundy married Carole Ann Boone. He took advantage of an existing Florida statute in which a marriage declaration in court in front of a judge constituted a legal marriage. Thus, Bundy called Boone as a character witness and married her while she was on the witness stand. After numerous conjugal visits, Boone gave birth to a daughter in October 1982. She returned to Washington in 1986 with her daughter after divorcing him and never returned.

Ann Rule described Bundy as "... a sadistic sociopath who took pleasure from another human's pain and the control he had over his victims, to the point of death, and even after." He once referred to himself as "the most cold-hearted son of a bitch you'll ever meet" and one of his defense attorneys, Polly Nelson, said that Bundy "was the very definition of heartless evil." At one point, Bundy said, "We serial killers are your sons, we are your husbands, we are everywhere. And there will be more of your children dead tomorrow."

Bundy contacted Robert Keppel—the detective who helped put him in prison—while on death row to assist him with the "Green River Killer" investigation at the time. With Bundy's assistance, Keppel was able to understand the inner workings of the mind of a serial killer and was, subsequently, able to identify and apprehend Gary Ridgway in November 2001.

Ted Bundy has been the subject of three television movies and one feature film. The two-part film entitled *The Deliberate Stranger* aired on NBC in 1986, starring Mark Harmon as Bundy. *Ted Bundy* (2002) starred Michael Reilly Burke as Bundy and was directed by Matthew Bright. In 2003 the USA Network aired Ann Rule's *The Stranger Beside Me* that starred Billy Campbell as Bundy and Barbara Hershey as Rule. Finally, the A&E network produced an adaptation of detective Robert Keppel's book *The Riverman* in 2004, starring Cary Elwes as Bundy and Bruce Greenwood as Keppel.

LOUISA MERRIFIED : POISON KILLER

136

ANA BENSON

Louisa Merrifield Biography

There is an ongoing myth that if a woman wants to murder someone, she will use poison. These claims are partially true because 40% of killers who used poison are female. Surely, women do have more opportunities to administer the dangerous concoction to their victims because they are the caregivers. The women cook food, take care of a household, etc. And in the past, poison was simply laying around in forms of different cleaning agents and rodenticides.

The poisoners would often benefit from their victim's death, and this happened in the case of Louisa Merrifield, also known as the Blackpool Poisoner. She wanted to inherit a nice property in a wealthy part of the town, and Sarah Ricketts was in her way.

Early life

Louisa May was born in 1909 in Wigan, United Kingdom. Her father was a Methodist minister while her mother stayed at home in order to take care of the family. Louisa May grew up in a very religious environment, and her father was quite strict. She didn't have the freedom to do what she wanted which resulted in Louisa's unhappy adolescence. The same feeling stayed with her throughout her life. Louisa May didn't finish school so she didn't get the proper education which could have improved her status. After all, her father didn't allow it because it was uncommon for girls to attend colleges back in the day. Louisa May was supposed to be just like her mother and manage the household.

Louisa was very unlucky in terms of the relationships as well. She wasn't an attractive woman. As a matter of fact, Louisa was short and stocky, so there weren't a lot of suitors coming her way. But she did marry a man called Joseph who was an ironworker. Joseph was a heavy drinker who would spend the majority of his days either at work or in a local pub. The couple had four children together. The marriage lasted until Joseph's death from liver failure. His body simply couldn't take the amount of alcohol he drank regularly. Louisa hated being married to Joseph, and she eventually admitted to her friends that she felt relieved when he died.

It took Louisa only three months to find a new husband. The recent widow chose her lodger who was seventy-eight years old. Louisa was in her thirties, but she clearly wasn't bothered by this age difference. The lodger's name was Richard Watson, and the two were married for only two months. Richard suffered a fatal heart attack, making Louisa a widow for the second time. Having in mind the events that would occur later, some investigators did take a closer look at Richard's death but found nothing suspicious about it. The man was almost eighty years old, and it is very likely that he died from natural causes.

Louisa May wasn't a wealthy woman, but she longed for the money and the easy life. She often struggled to put the food on the table and wanted to provide the necessities to all of her four children. Since she couldn't find a way to earn more money from her work, Louisa decided to commit a ration book fraud. The entire country was in the war, and the supplies were sparse. Ration books were used in order to even the field and provide every family with just enough food, clothes, and other useful goods. But Louisa wasn't happy with the amount her family was getting. So she managed to put her hands on a total of seven ration books, giving her more than enough supplies. However, her crime was soon discovered which lead to a quick arrest.

The war was coming to an end, and the United Kingdom started dealing with the criminals who abused the post-conflict situation in the country. Louisa May was sentenced to 84 days in prison and she was locked up in 1946. That wasn't the end of her ordeal because as soon as she was released, three of her children were taken away from her. The government decided that she was an unfit mother and that the children should be placed in the institutions because they will give them all the care they needed. Left on her own, Louisa May felt lost. With two failed marriages behind her, she started thinking about tying the knot once again.

Marriage to Alfred Merrifield

Louisa May was forty-six years old when she decided to marry Alfred Merrifield. He lived in Blackpool and was a pensioner. Alfred was significantly older than Louisa and he was in his sixties. The man was in good health, except for the fact that he was slightly deaf. It is suspected that Louisa selected Alfred because she thought that there is no way someone her age would be interested in her. As previously mentioned, she considered herself to be below average when it comes to physical appearance, and the years haven't been kind to her either. She was a bit overweight and starting to lose her sight. Louisa had to wear thick eyeglasses in order to function properly.

Alfred was a mild-mannered man who liked Louisa a lot. She would later tell her friends that Alfred pursued her for months until she finally agreed to become his wife. It was clear that Alfred's money wasn't the motivation because his overall income was very low. The newlyweds struggled a lot from the very beginning of their marriage. The financial problems weren't something uncommon for Louisa, so she did her best to find more work. Alfred tried to help her out a bit, but no one would offer him any temporary work position.

The only thing Louisa did well was housekeeping. After all, she did take care of her family for years. She applied for various cooking jobs, as well as for nursing positions, but she would often get fired. Her past employers described her as a difficult woman who would often argue with her supervisors. Louisa also drank a lot, which was a habit she picked up from her first husband. Alfred and Louisa simply couldn't make things work when it came to the finances. His pension was too low, and she kept losing the jobs. In the end, they started selling or pawning their possessions in hopes they would be able to survive a month. It was a difficult life filled with ups and downs. They needed a break as soon as possible because worrying if they will have enough money to buy food next week was tiring. Therefore, Louisa Merrifield grabbed the local newspapers in hopes of finding any type of work that would fit her experience and qualifications. She saw an interesting ad in Lancashire Evening Gazette, and things quickly moved forward.

Meeting Sarah Ricketts

Blackpool is a well-known vacation spot in the United Kingdom. Overall, the city is quite wealthy due to the tourists who frequent this place in the warmer months. Sarah Ricketts was a middle-class woman and a widow. She lived alone in a bungalow in Blackpool, which was located at 339 Devonshire Road. The house was in a part of the city called Norbreck which housed many prominent families that lived in the area. The woman had plenty of money and could afford to have a live-in housekeeper who would take care of both her and the household. Sarah was disabled, and she needed help as well as the company. Considering the location and the terms, Sarah Ricketts expected that many people would respond to her newspaper ad. She was looking for a housekeeper and a handyman who would live on her property.

But Sarah was infamous for her behavior, and the majority of candidates were not willing to deal with her. As previously stated, she had plenty of money in her bank account, but Sarah still acted like a middle-class woman. The widow was quite short and tiny, but she would intimidate anyone around her with her fiery temper. She was a difficult woman, and her dietary habits were particularly strange. As a matter of fact, she loved to eat jam, often straight out of the jar. Afterwards, she would have rum and stout. Having in mind that Sarah Ricketts was seventy-nine years old, her food preferences were very odd.

Sarah Ricketts needed reliable help around the house, and as she was reviewing the applications, Louisa Merrifield's immediately stood out. She was married to Alfred Merrifield so Sarah thought that he would be a great addition to the household as well. After all, he would be able to fix things around the bungalow. Sarah didn't know that Louisa Merrifield had a sketchy history. It was omitted from the application because Louisa's goal was to present herself in the best possible light. Sarah's rushed decision eventually had terrible consequences.

Louisa and Alfred Merrifield accepted Sarah's invitation to work for her, and the couple arrived at the bungalow on 12th March 1953. Things were looking great in the first couple of weeks, and Sarah was happy with her choice. Louisa was fairly young and able to take care of Sarah. Her cooking was great, and Sarah enjoyed the meals Louisa would prepare on a daily basis. Alfred was in charge of the gardening, and he cleared out the overgrown area, making the front yard beautiful once again. Sarah was ecstatic, and she started trusting her live-in housemates.

The entire neighborhood knew how happy Sarah was with her choice because she didn't hesitate to talk about them to her friends. She even gave Louisa her checkbook in order to pay the bills without thinking twice about the possibility that the woman might abuse this power, and steal her money. But the tensions started to rise very soon. Sarah began complaining that Louisa is not feeding her well. Apparently, Louisa's meals were starting to get sparse and Sarah was used to eating more food. She attacked Louisa that she was spending the food money on alcohol instead of buying quality ingredients for the kitchen.

The arguments were frequent, but this didn't stop Louisa and Alfred to approach Sarah's family doctor. Louisa was certain that Sarah liked her and appreciated the help she had provided so far. Apparently, the elderly lady wanted to write a new will, and she needed to get the doctor's permission that she is sane and clear-minded. The doctor was taken aback by this request, but having in mind that Sarah Ricketts lived alone and had two estranged daughters, he thought that she really liked her new housekeepers, and felt the need to leave them her bungalow, as well as the rest of the property. The bungalow was worth £3000, which is somewhere around $119,000 in today's currency.

The woman seemed coherent, and her solicitor was summoned to her bungalow as well. Sarah told him that Alfred and Louisa were good people who deeply cared about her wellbeing and that she wishes to leave them her property. She thought they do an excellent job around the house regardless of their tiny quarrels and that they deserve to inherit the property after her death. The solicitor wrote down the changes. Since he didn't sense any danger behind this request and the woman seemed completely sane, the doctor gave his approval, and a new will was made on 9th April 1953.

Sarah had a tendency to change her testament every now and then because she was often getting into fights with her two adult daughters. The woman thought they were after her money and would do her best to blackmail the two by denying them the property. As soon as Sarah Ricketts made a new will, Louisa started plotting how to kill the elderly woman. She traveled all the way to Manchester with her husband in order to get the things she needed and put her plan into motion. Alfred was very friendly to the clerk who worked at the store, and the man remembered him afterward. The two of them talked about health problems, including Alfred's deafness. The clerk didn't ask them where they were from, but the fact that they traveled for an hour to buy rat poison which is sold almost everywhere might have raised a flag right there on the spot.

The poison was a powerful concoction called Rodine, and it was used for eliminating rats from the households. The poison itself is quite strong due to the amount of white phosphorous it used to contain back in the days. Rodine is still sold today, but the formula had drastically changed. White phosphorous can be found in different military weapons, such as incendiary munition because it burns brightly and quickly. It can be quite damaging to humans, especially if one ingests it. As a matter of fact, 15mg of white phosphorous is enough to kill an adult. It is very toxic and can damage liver, heart, and kidneys. White phosphorous can be easily detected because the body might give a bit of a glow if someone managed to get this chemical into their system. The majority of people will notice a strong smell of garlic around white phosphorous as well. Rodine was a popular way of getting rid of rats, mostly due to its efficiency, so having it around the house wasn't an unusual thing.

The poisoning

Things really started to change during April because Louisa was quite unhappy with her job. She started complaining to everyone who would listen to her about how difficult Sarah Ricketts was. As a matter of fact, Louisa painted her as a very complicated person who would complain about the smallest things. Since the woman was partially paralyzed, she didn't move around too often. However, Louisa told her acquaintances that Sarah would simply ignore the fact that she cannot walk on her own and call them up in the middle of the night because she needed help getting out of the bed. Louisa was also annoyed because Sarah told her that her cooking was horrible, and she eventually started refusing to eat altogether.

Louisa was apparently disappointed in Sarah because she told the delivery man who brought her a supply of alcohol that the couple was spending too much money on themselves and that she would very likely fire them soon. Louisa claimed that wasn't true, and that Sarah was simply being mean to them even though they were doing their best to provide her with the best care possible. The following days were very confusing because Louisa mentioned to a couple of neighbors that Sarah died. It was evident that she was still alive and in the house.

When confronted with making false claims, Louisa simply told her friends: *"She's not dead yet, but she soon will be."* Surely enough, her sinister predictions will come true more sooner than later.

It was 13th of April when Louisa Merrifield decided that it was time to remove Sarah Ricketts from the picture. She prepared Sarah favorite meal and added a couple of spoons of Rodine to the jam. The woman started feeling sick right away because the dosage was very strong. As a matter of fact, Sarah was in unbelievable pain minutes after her meal. Unable to figure out what was going on, Sarah thought that she might be having digestion problems. Louisa helped her get to the bathroom, but Sarah was not feeling any better. She cried while in there, and her screams could be heard throughout the bungalow. Four hours have gone by, and Sarah completely lost the power of speech, unable to scream or speak to anyone. Five hours later Sarah Ricketts passed away. She died on 14th April 1953.

Louisa contacted Doctor Wood in order to report that Sarah is not feeling well. She didn't specify what exactly was happening with the woman. Even though Sarah Ricketts was old, she was fairly healthy. The woman didn't suffer from any chronic diseases, and the only thing that was sometimes problematic was bronchitis. However, it wasn't that frequent, so Doctor Wood didn't visit Sarah's home often. Since there was no hurry, the doctor decided to postpone his visit to the Ricketts' residence. But surprisingly, Sarah died the following morning. Knowing her history, Doctor Wood was certain right away that something was wrong. Yes, the woman was in her eighties, but she was perfectly fine the last time he examined her.

His suspicions were supported by Doctor Yule, who did a check-up on Sarah only a couple of days prior to her death because the housekeepers were asking for an approval in order to modify the woman's will. He asked the Merrifields what happened, and Louisa admitted that Sarah started feeling ill one day before her death, but she decided to contact Doctor Wood instead. According to her, she thought that he might feel agitated due to the fact that he already examined Sarah Ricketts recently. Louisa didn't fail to mention that Sarah wished to be cremated as soon as possible after her death. Doctor Yule found this even more strange because he knew the woman, and she never expressed her willingness to be sent away like that.

The autopsy

The entire situation was getting stranger as the more information came his way. Doctor Yule decided not to cremate Sarah's body, but to analyze it thoroughly instead. The law back then was not to issue a death certificate if anything seemed suspicious. The symptoms which were described by Louisa were very odd, and he needed to confirm that the woman wasn't killed. Doctor Yule decided to send Sarah's body to a coroner who would do a full autopsy.

After testing the tissues for any trace of poison, the coroner discovered high levels of white phosphorous in her liver. When he opened up the body, the internal organs had a faint glow to them which was quite alarming. Not to forget the garlic odor that filled out the room. This confirmed that Sarah died of phosphorous poisoning. Doctor Yule's concerns were confirmed, and now he knew that Sarah Ricketts was poisoned. He immediately alerted the authorities who zeroed in on her caretakers because they were always in contact with the woman, and had numerous opportunities to poison Sarah. After all, they were cooking her the meals and preparing food on a daily basis.

The investigation

Louisa and Alfred Merrifield worked for Sarah Ricketts for just over a month, and the woman clearly didn't know them well. They were the prime suspects from the very beginning, so the police started monitoring their steps very carefully. There were so many details that indicated that something was very wrong with Sarah's death. For instance, Louisa didn't feel sad when the woman passed away. Unsurprisingly to the law enforcement, she was excited because the bungalow belonged to her. Louisa was happy so she would constantly brag to her friends. Having in mind the peculiar way Sarah Ricketts died, the reporters approached Louisa a couple of weeks later to ask for a statement. She mostly focused on how much she disliked her husband, and that he was very boring. Louisa even implicated that he might have had an affair with Sarah which was completely untrue.

The police were familiar with the poison which was used in this murder, so they decided to search the bungalow in order to confirm it was available to Louisa Merrifield. After combing through the financial statements, they have discovered that the couple traveled to Manchester a few days before the murder. The police located the shop in which Rodine was bought, and they talked to the clerk who remembered talking to Alfred on that day. But this was still pretty normal due to the fact that numerous people used Rodine every single day. But knowing that the couple bought a full can of this poison gave them an advantage. The investigators thought that there should be more Rodine left in the bungalow because there is no need to use a whole can in just a couple of weeks. The poison is very efficient, and the can should still be in the bungalow unless they were covering up their tracks and getting rid of the evidence.

After a thorough search of the premises, the police officers didn't find a can of Rodine which suggested that the couple has thrown it away in hopes of not being discovered. Louisa and Alfred were in serious trouble because they remained the only suspects, and the police decided to arrest them right away. All the evidence were against them, and the fact that the United Kingdom still had a death penalty indicated that they might be facing this punishment.

The arrests and trial

Both Louisa and Alfred were brought to the station soon after the search of the bungalow was complete. When presented with the evidence, the investigators saw a change in Louisa's behavior. They told her about numerous interviews that proved she had talked about the death of Sarah Ricketts even before the poison was administered. Louisa tried blaming her husband, but this plan didn't work out well either. During Alfred's interview, the investigators did think that the old man was forced to follow Louisa's lead. He was deaf, and couldn't remember some of the key details of the whole incident. While the majority of detectives might think that the man was trying to save himself from the death sentence, the investigators working on this case actually believed that Alfred had little knowledge of the crime before it occurred.

Louisa and Alfred were brought to trial in July of 1953. Louisa defended herself by saying that Alfred cheated on her with Sarah Ricketts and that the two of them had a sexual relationship. Alfred once again had no knowledge of this, and the judge was certain that the man wasn't involved in the murder plot. Louisa continued to incriminate herself even further by refusing to admit that she talked about Sarah's death days before it really happened. However, multiple witnesses have confirmed this, and it was improbable that more than one person misheard her. Not to forget Louisa's behavior after Sarah's death.

The trial lasted for a total of nine days, and Louisa stuck to her defense that Alfred was having an affair with Sarah. However, the judge dismissed these claims, saying that Louisa is 'a vulgar and stupid woman with a dirty mind.' Louisa was found guilty of a first-degree murder and was sentenced to a death penalty by hanging. The judge was unsure what to do with Alfred because it was obvious that the old man didn't participate in the planning or the execution of the murder. In the end, the judge decided to drop the charges against Alfred Merrifield.

The aftermath

The public all around the United Kingdom wanted to know more about the Blackpool Poisoner, which was the nickname given to Louisa by the press. Everyone eagerly waited to hear what Alfred had to say about the murder and his wife Louisa. Since he was named as a beneficiary in Sarah's will, Alfred moved into the bungalow because it now legally belonged to him. He agreed to give an interview to national newspapers in which he talked about his marriage to Louisa. He admitted that he was very afraid for his own life because she had taken out a total of seven insurance policies on him. He was certain that she would have poisoned him as well if she wasn't in prison. Not to forget that Alfred admitted that Louisa abused him during their marriage which resulted in his bad health.

__ ...errifield was held in Strangeways Prison in Manchester. The judge has sent an official letter to the most famous hangman in the United Kingdom, and his name was Albert Pierrepoint. Pierrepoint accepted to be Louisa's executioner. He was experienced and didn't hesitate to execute women. The death penalty took place on 18th of September 1953 which was six months after the murder. She was the last woman hanged at Strangeways Prison. Louisa was buried inside the prison walls. Alfred did visit her twice before her death.

Alfred Merrifield continued living in Sarah Ricketts' bungalow for years after the poisoning, but the court ordered him to move out eventually. He continued to struggle financially and even appeared in local sideshows a couple of times. Alfred was eighty years old when he died in 1962.

THE TRAILSIDE KILLER

www.ingramcontent.com/pod-product-compliance
Lightning Source LLC
Chambersburg PA
CBHW022131150726
47992CB00002B/548